D1648983

The Decline
of
Rural Minnesota

Pipestone Community
Library

The Decline
of
Rural Minnesota

by
Joseph Amato
and
John W. Meyer

Marshall CROSSINGS PRESS *Minnesota*

The Decline of Rural Minnesota is a Crossings Press publication.

Published in cooperation with The Society for the Study of Local and Regional History, Marshall, Minnesota.

The 1874 map on the cover was furnished by Donata DeBruyckere.

All rights reserved. No part of this publication may be reproduced in any form without permission in writing from the publisher.

Copyright © 1993 by Crossings Press

Published and distributed in the United States of America by:

Crossings Press
P.O. Box 764
Marshall, MN 56258

ISBN 0-9614119-6-1
Printed and bound in the United States of America

The paper used in this publication meets the requirements of the American National Standard for Permanence of Paper for Printed Library Materials Z39.48-1984.

Table of Contents

Acknowledgments

This book had its beginning in a 1988 invitation by the League of Minnesota Cities to address the annual conference celebrating their seventy-fifth anniversary. They asked me for a report on the condition of rural Minnesota. Reluctantly, I agreed ... on the condition that they recognize that I was not a trained demographer and that my generalizations about rural Minnesota would primarily be based on what I knew about southwestern Minnesota, which meant for me either the agricultural region that surrounds Marshall, Minnesota, west of the Minnesota River, or the 19 southwestern counties of the state: Brown, Chippewa, Cottonwood, Jackson, Kandiyohi, Lac Qui Parle, Lincoln, Lyon, Martin, Meeker, Murray, Nobles, Pipestone, Redwood, Renville, Rock, Swift, Watonwan, and Yellow Medicine.

The League accepted my conditions, and I set to work consolidating what I had learned from twenty years of experience and observation of rural Minnesota. I knew how regional towns and cities were losing their autonomy as human communities and, even in cases when their populations did not decrease, they functioned more and more as suburbs of nearby lead cities and colonial outposts of the Twin Cities. I also knew that farms which prospered grew, if not dramatically, relentlessly larger, while the size of farm families themselves diminished. I was aware that rural wages were low and opportunities were few for the young, especially the talented young, who migrated in increasing numbers. Although I didn't know the exact numbers, the graying of rural Minnesota stood out clearly as regional newspapers weekly reported more deaths than births, the closing of stores and schools, and the opening of nursing homes and facilities for the elderly.

The more I reflected on the diverse forms of rural decline, the more I became conscious of how it involved all facets of rural society—not just its demography and economy, but its politics and culture. I could not separate rural Minnesota's decline from the patterns stemming from the national settlement period of the Midwest after the Civil War, nor from the eclipse of agricultural and rural societies throughout the world during the past two centuries. The combination of such factors as aging populations, the loss of the autonomy of local institutions, and diminishing numbers of farms and farmers (a process exacerbated by the farm crisis of the 1980s) pushed me in the direction of believing that Minnesota's rural life, as incorporated approximately a century and a half earlier, was approaching its end.

With a mixture of historical insight, everyday intuition, and basic numbers, I found myself formulating pessimistic conclusions. My friend Ted Radzilowski encouraged me to go where my thoughts led, even if they proved unpopular. University of Minnesota geographer John Borchert, who generously agreed to read an early draft of my address, assured me that I was not off track. Believing that boosterism was the orthodoxy of the contemporary countryside, I was pleasantly surprised by how well my pessimistic address was received at the League's convention. However, a few months later when the League published my address in their monthly *Minnesota Cities*, I breathed a sigh of relief, believing my interlude as a "prophet" of the future of rural Minnesota was over, and I could get back to the solid ground of European cultural and intellectual history.

Acknowledgments

So things remained until Deb Nyberg, the new editor of the League's publication *Minnesota Cities*, asked me to write several more articles. Flattered and paid, I again took up the prophet's mantle, producing during the next two years the handful of articles on the demographic, social, and cultural decline of rural Minnesota which became the heart of this book.

Because of the range of approaches, especially those involving quantitative methods, I could not have done this book without the help of John Meyer, friend, fellow golfer, Canby city manager, and rural sociologist. In the fullest sense of the word, John is co-author of two of the most important chapters in this book. The chapter on natural decline rests on his singular observation of what happened in parts of rural Minnesota between 1985 and 1990. His insights shaped much of the chapter on the changing character of leadership in contemporary rural Minnesota. His experience, ideas, observations, and analysis were also helpful at many other points in the book, and he singularly encouraged me to push my intuitional and anecdotal approach into territories where I would never have ventured on my own.

In addition to my gratitude to John, my thanks go to John's wife, Mary, and their six children, and my wife, Catherine, and our four children. Families pay for books with the most important human currencies.

Additionally, special thanks go to former League executive director Don Slater, who consistently encouraged me by repeatedly suggesting, "Say what you're saying. No one else is." I also thank Jean Goad, who has edited *Minnesota Cities* during the last several years.

In Marshall, former mayor John Feda and city administrators Duane Aden and Cal Barnett have been insightful, as was my friend, attorney Kevin Stroup of Clarkfield. At Southwest State University, I thank Kathy Wilking and Arlene Schoephoester of the word processing department. Over the years I have learned to count on them to work hard and kibitz well. As in the past, thanks are also due to Donata DeBruyckere of the university's rural studies program and Jan Louwagie of the university's history center. They are friends, fellow workers, and founders of the Society for the Study of Local and Regional History.

My friend John Radzilowski, whose *Out on the Wind: The Poles and Danes in Lincoln County, Minnesota, 1880–1905* was published by Crossings Press, proved an excellent copy editor. Kathy Wenzel of Livewire Printing Co. of Jackson, Minnesota, also deserves strong thanks. As book designer and producer, she repeatedly proved her good nature, intelligence, and creativity.

Finally, I wish to thank a variety of audiences brought together by the League of Minnesota Cities, Department of Trade and Economic Development, the Minnesota Humanities Commission, and the Countryside Council. They listened to me speak about aspects of decline in rural Minnesota without once using the term pessimist to silence me even when I dared to say of rural Minnesota (as quoted by the Associated Press), "there is a backlog of death out here," and "I think it is possible that a form of civilization is dying . . . , a civilization that is only 125 years old."

I can only say to those who have listened to my ideas and now read this book, now it is your turn. Take up this book, and read, discuss, and criticize it as you wish. There is no orthodoxy here other than belief that rural Minnesota deserves the truth as best we can get it.

Foreword

Joseph Amato has been teaching history and rural studies at Southwest State University in Marshall, Minnesota, for more than two decades. He possesses a restless curiosity, with an imagination that reaches from the most detailed facts of local history to the most abstract ideas of philosophy. He is an intellectual who has not merely survived, but flourished, on the prairie.

With Canby city administrator John Meyer, Amato has written a series of separate articles over the course of several years for the League of Minnesota Cities. In gathering these articles in the book, *The Decline of Rural Minnesota*, Amato and Meyer have performed a valuable service in raising many provocative questions about contemporary rural Minnesota.

What has aroused the most attention is Amato and Meyer's identification of "natural population decline"—a situation in which deaths exceed births—in twelve rural Minnesota counties during the 1980s. But Amato and Meyer also lay out a number of other basic trends in rural Minnesota, especially the southwest region: a shrinking and aging population, diminishing economic resources, weakened political influence, the emigration of the young and the talented, and a decline in business and civic leadership.

They do more than simply report these trends. They situate them in the context of a larger story about a metropolitan civilization which advanced onto the prairies and plains but which now seems to be receding. The story that Amato and Meyer tell is rich with implications. Readers can draw their own conclusions, but there are three issues on which I would focus.

The interdependence of countryside and city.

Professor Amato is the author of another fascinating small book, published in 1980, entitled *Countryside: Mirror of Ourselves.* In it, he concludes that "we have all increasingly become conscious of how much 'the countryside' is for us a matter of myth and argument, interpretation and debate. . . . We speak of the countryside as one when in fact there is no one countryside. There are many countrysides, each subject to different forms of change, each having a separate history. For reasons of nostalgia, politics or personal eccentricity, we often insist on a single countryside—be it that of single living black earth worthy of reverence or a hard, sterile rock needing attack, the land of our own people."

There is, by almost any measure, considerable diversity among rural areas within the United States as well as within Minnesota itself. For example, Minnesota has within its borders both some of the richest and some of the poorest rural counties in America. On balance, compared to many other regions in the United States, in the Midwest there has been a remarkable persistence of family farming along with the "traditional" way of life that supposedly goes along with it. Yet, the average "family farm" in Minnesota today is several times larger than the average "family farm" of just a few decades ago. The same piece of land that once supported several families now supports one (and even then often requires an off-farm supplementary income).

In the span of about 125 years, rural Minnesota has risen and fallen. Some areas have risen more than others; some have fallen more than others. People can argue about whether "mobility" is a good or bad thing. But nobody can argue, at least in the American context, that mobility is a new phenomenon. In many respects, rural Minnesota is a story about migrations. The countryside was populated by a mobile people, and it is now being depopulated by a mobile people.

"Rural Minnesota" did not exist until people came to settle the land; to make a livelihood; to establish villages and towns to conduct their economic, political, social, and spiritual lives. In other words, rural Minnesota is an unnatural act. It is a creation of, first, the railroads and, then, the highways—and, always, of the cities that consumed what the settlers on the land produced for them.

As Amato has pointed out, "the countryside" is ultimately a construct of the imagination—one that is almost always constructed in opposition to the city. This struggle between the center and the periphery, the city and the countryside, is a familiar story. It is a struggle, however, that does not come from the separation and isolation of the two but from their connection and interdependence. According to historian William Cronon, "Americans have long tended to see city and country as separate places, more isolated from each other than connected. We carefully partition our national landscape into urban places, rural places, and wilderness. Although we often cross the symbolic boundaries between them—seeking escape or excitement, recreation or renewal—we rarely reflect on how tightly bound together they really are."

In *Nature's Metropolis*, his fascinating study of the concomitant rise of Chicago and the rural Midwest, Cronon concludes: "We all live in the city. We all live in the country. Both are second nature to us. . . . To do right by nature and people in the country, one has to do right by them in the city as well, for the two seem always to find in each other their own image. In that sense, every city is nature's metropolis, and every piece of countryside its rural hinterland. We fool ourselves if we think we can choose between them, for the green lake and orange cloud are creatures of the same landscape. Each is our responsibility. We can only take them together and, in making the journey between them, find a way of life that does justice to them both."

The challenge of leadership.

Amato and Meyer emphasize the social psychology of the many profound changes currently taking place on the countryside. If decline is real and inevitable, what does this mean for both the reality and the feeling of community in rural Minnesota? Can rural communities establish larger alliances or bring a vision to their regions? How do we talk sensibly and critically about these matters? Can rural Minnesota live gracefully with its decline? How should rural institutions and leaders respond? With despair and resignation? With a fit of boosterism? With a clear-eyed acknowledgment of the positives and negatives?

Someone has suggested that "rural development" is a self-contradiction. Whether public or private, attempts at rural development have too often been moved by greed, incompetence, or wishful thinking—wasting the time, money, and hopes of too many individuals and communities. The hopes for investment—not to mention loyalty, solidarity, and community spirit—seem to be getting bleaker. Amato and Meyer ask the question that many rural residents have already asked in their own personal lives: "How do you put down roots where there is no long-term promise of work or home?" Rural Minnesotans may now be even more mobile than their city cousins, who have long been stereotyped as the rootless wanderers.

There are, of course, plenty of leaders in rural Minnesota proposing their own solutions. There is still no shortage of the traditional boosters, seemingly oblivious to all that goes on around them. Second, there are the technocratic leaders who promise that the miracles of new information and communications technology will revive rural areas. They propose a kind of social cryonics—try to freeze a dying countryside until the technology is developed to save it. Third, there are the moralistic leaders who believe their rural communities are declining because they represent the last refuge of decency and virtue in an increasingly corrupt and decaying world—at least a consolation, if not a solution. Finally, there are the many political leaders who still try to cut deals at the state legislature to get the last piece of bacon for their district, county, or town—in what usually amounts to a zero-sum competition against their neighbors.

What rural Minnesota needs above all—and they do exist—are leaders who are willing to ask questions first; leaders who are then willing to search for answers which they realize may never be found; leaders who will speak frankly to citizens about the challenges they confront together; leaders who will seek to overcome the inertia of bureaucracy and conventional opinion.

The need for critical analysis of our institutions.

Finally, if our institutions and our leaders (and ordinary citizens)—whether urban or rural or somewhere in between—are to make sound decisions, then they need good information. *The Decline of Rural Minnesota* highlights the need for critical analysis of our institutions and how they are functioning.

We need to look at educational institutions (both K–12 and post-secondary); the health care system; the various agencies of state, county, and municipal units of government; businesses; churches; social service organizations; libraries; and print and electronic media. All of these should be regularly subjected to critical evaluation—not just from within and not just from an academic perspective.

We should always be asking: Are these institutions really functioning as they should be? Are they really doing what they claim to be doing? A democratic society needs critical intelligence applied to its own institutions. Of course, it is true that we already get occasional journalistic reports, government memos, and academic studies. What I would propose, however, is a working group that might draw on the talents of, say, a historian, a political scientist, an economist, a geographer, an anthropologist, and an artist—along with an independent-minded government administrator, a lawyer, a businessperson, and a thoughtful politician. Throw in a teacher, a librarian, and a journalist for good measure.

The purpose of such a working group would not be to repeat the conventional wisdom or to mold some cherished "consensus." Instead, it should provide analysis, both comprehensive and critical, that could reinvigorate public discourse about our state and its institutions. This working group could produce research and commentary, as well as recommendations for reform and legislation. It would be an analysis that is provocative and accessible to the public, yet based on solid intellectual work. (This would mean offering comparisons across time and place—that is, historical analysis as well as comparisons with other states, even other countries. Yes, it is possible that our institutions might actually be able to learn something from other times, other places.)

Ideally, such a working group would not turn away from unpleasant truths, nor be afraid to challenge vested interests. Its work would be intellectually honest and practical-minded. We desperately need people who are willing to raise hard questions and unwilling to settle for easy answers. (The need is no less great in urban areas than it is in rural areas.) In other words, we need much more of precisely what Amato and Meyer provide in these essays.

Nobody would accuse Amato and Meyer of viewing the rural world through rose-colored glasses. Others will see things differently. That is fine. But we need Amato and Meyer's perspective, too. Amato himself has always insisted that we must tell stories about ourselves, and some stories will inevitably conflict with others. With *The Decline of Rural Minnesota*, Amato and Meyer tell a fascinating story from which even its critical readers can learn.

—Ross Corson, Minneapolis

◆

Ross Corson is Executive Assistant to Walter F. Mondale, the U.S. Ambassador to Japan. He previously worked for the DFL Education Foundation and the Countryside Council (based in Marshall, Minnesota).

Preface

In August 1969, my wife, my two children (soon to number four) and I moved to Cottonwood, Minnesota, a village of 800 inhabitants, thirteen miles north of Marshall. I had just gotten a college position teaching history at the new four-year college in Marshall. Unlike my wife, I had no previous experience living in a small town, which I promptly demonstrated by violating a cardinal rule of small-town politics. I ran for school board my first year in town. This resulted in a monumental voter turn-out, and I suffered a resounding defeat. I took a drubbing and learned just how seriously these people—no doubt agitated by the national protests of the late 1960s—defended their schools, especially when they were threatened by an outsider, and no ordinary outsider, either, but a member of what was popularly understood to be that drug-laden, hippie-filled, war-protesting college just a few miles to the south. I had been given a quick lesson in how ferocious the wrath of a threatened superintendent and his scared teachers can be: their kingdom was not meant to be changed.

My second lesson in rural life came when I formed and headed a group to study Lake Cottonwood. I was able to do this thanks to the acceptance of a handful of the town's leaders, especially Bror Anderson, who was the head of Cottonwood's major employer, North Star Insurance, and of Cottonwood's active

9

Lions Club. The lake study, which had a modest budget of a few thousand dollars, produced a report for the community and gave me an education in just how many state and regional jurisdictions and agencies can converge in any particular spot, blocking all hope of change.

My third lesson was the privilege of watching close up the creative social work of Father Denis Becker of Cottonwood's St. Mary's Catholic Church. Becker was intelligent and extraordinarily gregarious, and he was one of those odd individuals who truly liked other people. One of the first things Becker did was offer his many-bedroomed and well-equipped priest home to the incoming minister of Christ Lutheran Church who, along with his large family, was without a place to stay until a new rectory was completed. Christ Lutheran not only graciously accepted Becker's kind invitation, but Bror and his wife, Trudy, invited Becker to stay with them. Which he did. This act of mutual goodwill taught the community about acceptance.

A town whose anti-foreign and anti-Catholic sentiments allegedly landed the foundation stones of St. Mary's in the lake and produced a handful of KKK members was now officially open to Catholics. The Catholics of St. Mary's, composed primarily of the resented but increasingly successful Belgian Catholic farmers south of town, were now accepted as part of a Norwegian Lutheran community.

In defiance of Bishop Alphonse Schladweiler's warning, Becker ran and got himself elected mayor of Cottonwood. No sooner was he elected than Becker opened city meetings to all. He successfully led the town in its bid for a million-dollar HUD project.

Becker filled Cottonwood with new energy. The Lions Club thrived. Even after Becker left, as if his spirit had remained, the town's energy was positive. It first led to the building of a fine nine-hole golf course at the west end of the town and was followed by the building of several new housing developments.

Becker's successes came after I had formed my first judgments of the region. I transferred my views of the nation at large to the village. Sometime in 1966 I had concluded, despite what up to then had been my standing disinterest in politics, that the nation was pursuing a wrong-headed war in Vietnam. Two years in the smog-filled basin of southern California in the Riverside-San Bernardino area convinced me that the nation as a whole was on the wrong course. When my wife and I, just married, crossed the Mississippi at Winona in 1966 on the way to a university position in California, I was struck by the river's immensity. Three years later on the way to my new job in Marshall, again crossing the Mississippi at Winona, I was struck by how small, frail, and vulnerable this mighty river was. No doubt the oil spills on the beaches of Santa Barbara and thousands of sheep killed by a nerve gas accident at Dugway proving grounds in Utah had altered my consciousness.

I arrived in Cottonwood, disillusioned with the nation (as many young people were at the time). An experienced war protester, and not afraid to speak out, I was in Cottonwood hardly more than a year when I wrote my first commentary on southwest Minnesota in the form of a long letter to the Marshall *Independent*. Later, in October 1971, with modest revisions, I sent the same letter to Bishop Schladweiler, who had established a fund to help alleviate regional poverty.

I introduced my letter setting forth what I took to be the visible signs of the region's poverty and disorder: I noted, among other things, a disproportionate number of old people, with no source of income other than Social Security; dying towns, which steadily lost not only population but all their schools and businesses; an absence of good jobs; and a whole generation of youth who were emigrating because of low-paying jobs. I noted that regional companies paid only minimal wages ($1.60 an hour), that labor was almost universally non-unionized, and there existed a symbiotic relationship between inferior wages and welfare.

Regional leadership was narrow and limited. The newspapers expressed the opinion of the business class, whose conservative attitudes dominated the region. Prospering towns like Marshall didn't cooperate with surrounding towns. The college, churches, and other associations also did little to foster regional unity. The area had little consciousness of itself. Its leadership, old and fragmented, was tied to the outside world in matters of ideology, politics, and money. It had no vision of what people could and should accomplish together if they and the region were to have a future.

The educational system, I elaborated an additional point, did little to help this situation. The administrators, like almost everywhere, tended to follow rather than lead the community. The teachers accepted a passive role; their goals . . . to make a living, to avoid controversy and politics, to be discrete, and to have glory in preparing students to go on to college. In effect, they assured the exit of the brightest and most-needed youth.

I concluded with a list of problems that resembled on many counts those of an underdeveloped country: out-migration; inadequate compensation for our agricultural products; a lack of industry, regional cooperation, and progressive education; a fear of change and a sense of helplessness; an absence of capital circulation where money enters the region quickly, and exits more quickly, without generating real and substantial economic growth and benefits. The first thing required was consciousness that our region was economically depressed.

Bishop Schladweiler, Father Becker told me, simply didn't understand my letter. He didn't reply. Apparently, the notion that southwest Minnesota could be conceived as an underdeveloped country baffled the bishop.

More than ten years passed before I again reconsidered the region where I lived. The more local worlds wanted and needed, the more they sacrificed their freedom and autonomy to distant worlds of commerce and state. I increasingly concurred with the central thesis of Karl Polyani's book on nineteenth-century European society, *The Great Transformation:* The bigger the market, the bigger the state; and the bigger the market and state, the more they intervene in the countryside.

This anticipated a second idea on the region, which I called "more with less," and set forth as if it were a law: As the mass increases at the center, so do its functions, whereas while the functions increase at the periphery—as they must given the uniformity of the state and market—the mass decreases, leaving it to do more, with less. Short of people to carry out multiplying functions, the periphery must do—or at least must claim to do—more with less.

Increasing want and necessity registered in growing specialization and multiplying complexity at the center of the society. In turn, increasing functions, articulated by law, implemented by bureaucracies, and supported by rising and diversifying expectations, require rural institutions, at ever accelerating rates, to do more and more, with fewer people and less funds.

As the traditional economic theory of marginal returns suggests, there is a point in place and time at which there are too many people, or too many assets, for optimal production, so the converse may be argued in the case of the contemporary rural world which has too few people and assets seeking to do too many things in order to keep up with the multiplying functions of the metropolitan center. There is a point, to further mirror the theory of marginal returns, when there is so much to get done that nothing gets done at all. At the extreme, rural institutions now suffer a condition of "frenzied entropy."

A corresponding second point describes many rural public institutions. Routinely asked to do more than they possibly can, standard operating policy is to claim to do the impossible. Unless this commonplace institutional lying becomes a matter of public scrutiny, it goes unchallenged, for to do so would call attention to the dysfunctional relationship that exists between metropolis and periphery, between the demands of the legislature and state bureaucracy and local and regional resources.

Administrators are rotated frequently in the countryside (at least this is the case at Southwest State and the other state universities). Old administrators, exhausted by their diverse and conflicting assignments, run out of "old lies" to tell, while new administrators—at least temporarily—can tell the new lies the metropolis wants to hear. These shared lies create what vulgarly could be called a "bullshit concord," whose primary purpose (in addition to maintaining jobs for those involved) sustains and conceals the growing imbalance between metropolitan and periphery, legislature and rural institutions and people.

There was no problem grasping the elaboration and application of the law of more with less in the countryside. Indeed, it is met at every turn. It was alive and well at the university, where in my first ten years I taught a range of courses that an average university teacher wouldn't teach in a lifetime. I saw it in the functioning of a local teachers' union in which we took turns doing chores that large metropolitan unions would have whole staffs to do. It existed in the frequent condition of frenzied entropy of the university's administration which was forced to satisfy increasing contradictory demands from on high. There is no end to requests for reports, curriculum evaluations, and implementation of new social-moral directives. There are emotionally exhausting and crippling budgetary about-faces, spawned by changing administrative orders, a fluctuating economy, and the vagaries of bi-annual state legislation.

One hears similar stories from regional businesses, law offices, medical clinics, and farms, especially at tax time. They too agonize as they try to keep up with the increasing flood of laws, demands, and specializations that engulf their professions and lives. Some remark that they find themselves being outpaced by new technologies, increased paperwork, and ever-refined sensibilities in their own households. Few, if any, believe that new and labor-saving devices are doing away with older necessary functions faster than new functions are appearing. The farmer escapes being harnessed to a plow to be chained to a pencil. (Perhaps, somewhere in the universe, there is a malevolent angel who keeps the balance of human misery by making sure that the elimination of old and tedious physical chores are matched by the introduction of new mental agonies.)

A friend from the Twin Cities argued that people in the countryside weren't alone in suffering the condition of "more with less." He didn't elaborate—but I was humored by visions of Minneapolis falling behind Chicago; Chicago, New York; New York, Paris—specialist succumbing to specialist, up and down the line. Like dying stars, each metropolitan center collapsing back upon itself, returning the countryside to its original darkness. Such big, black visions aside, it humored me to think that we couldn't keep up with ourselves.

I intuitively believed—as I discovered a few others did as well—that the rate of specialization in our civilization exceeds the growth of population. The theory of "more with less" has an echo in the great American prophet of decline, Henry Adams. Adams' argument was that contemporary civilization's accumulating power causes change that outstrips thought itself. It leaves us without even metaphors of time to describe and value the path we follow. For Adams, the only appropriate symbol for the contemporary world was the dynamo itself.

Joseph Tainter, in *The Collapse of Complex Societies*, contends that civilizations lose themselves at their peripheries. Invariably, the number of profitable conquests decline and the logistics of control, transport, and communication involve ever-increasing costs of exploiting and governing its peripheries. Collapse for Tainter does not take the form of a singular catastrophe, but a gradual retreat to a condition of less complexity.

This applies to rural Minnesota. It is a periphery to which it is increasingly costly for the metropolitan centers of Minneapolis and St. Paul to deliver services and goods and implement the law. Geographer John Borchert admirably showed in *America's Northern Heartland* how rural Minnesota, North and South Dakota, and Montana were the children of the railroad lines of the Twin Cities which, in turn, were subordinate to greater economic and political hierarchies. In *Nature's Metropolis: Chicago and the Great West*, William Cronon argues that the commanding narrative of the nineteenth-century American west "was that of an expanding metropolitan economy creating ever more elaborate and intimate linkages between city and countryside."

For one short period in the two decades after the Civil War, the center lent the periphery its energy, along with its attention, hope, money, steel, and people. The Twin Cities, according to Borchert, reached out in every direction—to the northern forests and iron ranges, to the northern Great Plains, the Canadian prairies, and the Pacific northwest; the Iowa prairies and the distant mid-continent centers at Omaha, Kansas City and St. Louis; to Chicago-Milwaukee and the lesser lake ports such as Ashland, Sault Ste. Marie, and Green Bay. As forests were cut, mines dug, prairies fenced, and lakes drained, the countryside was the focus of great human plans and energy. Fundamental choices were made over the paths of railroad lines, the sites of railroad towns and county seats. In Minnesota, eighty-seven towns got the all-important designation of county seat and of them, to quote

16

Borchert, "less than 30 sites emerged as the state's diversified multi-county trade retail centers," and of those, "only seven arose as the state's main centers of wholesale trade, services, and industry as Minnesota moved into this century"—Minneapolis-Saint Paul, a preponderant first; Duluth second; followed by Winona, Mankato, St. Cloud, Bemidji, and Moorhead.

By 1890 a new civilization had established its outposts in the countryside, and rural Minnesota was its peripheral region. In ways it was similar to the new colonial and underdeveloped regions of the late nineteenth-century imperial era. Thereafter, decline would threaten if at any one point the metropolis lost interest or lacked means to integrate its peripheries into an ever more complex urban civilization.

The decline that stalked the countryside almost since its beginnings appeared forcefully in the 1980s. In that decade a significant farm crisis elevated population losses to twenty percent in Minnesota's most rural counties as emigration accelerated. Youth departed in increasing numbers, leaving behind an older population, which itself is establishing regional and national patterns of migration that are yet to be studied. Smaller towns (2,500 and below and even up to 5,000) age and lose population and autonomy. Agriculture, the primary industry of much of rural Minnesota, however prosperous, supports fewer and fewer people. Small retail businesses fail, main streets deteriorate, and the business classes—which once supplied leaders and a sense of town patriotism—vanish. As the rural tax base constricts—due to a loss of taxpayers and a loss of property value—both revenues and discretionary funds diminish. Financial dependency increases, while freedom and choice diminish. Public actions are reduced to reactions, causing fatalism and lethargy to grow. Rural Minnesota approaches the end of a way of life.

There never was a good reason to presume that the center would continue to invest unusual sums in the periphery. The spectacular funds invested in the west were a result of roughly three decades of British capital and U.S. capital and government bending their energies to opening the prairie. Also there never was a reason to presume that those on the agricultural periphery had the means to keep pace with the accelerating complexity of an expanding industrial civilization. Nevertheless, while the forward momentum of the countryside considerably slows, there remains an umbilical cord of laws, institutions, and wants that joins the periphery to the center.

The retreat of the metropolis from the countryside will not be sudden, but selective and political, and thus erratic, pell-mell, and incoherent. The private sector's withdrawal, already seen in abandonment of rail and bus lines, will be no more orderly. In all likelihood, in the future only regional centers will be seen to be worthy of voluntary public and private investment, and these centers will be more and more under the control of the distant agencies. Local authorities and autonomies, and local, regional, and traditional associations and cultures will be eclipsed.

Much of what was once culturally, socially, and politically unique in rural Minnesota will be demoted to the status of nostalgia. Cities and communities assembled on this prairie less than a century ago have now been overshadowed by a changing urban horizon. Peoples of this region will increasingly know and define themselves as migrants in a changing world rather than as members of fixed places and established communities. Similar to the settlers of this region, people will know themselves as much by their migrations as by their homes.

Hopefully, these essays will help the citizens of rural Minnesota to understand this great transformation at hand. Although this will not spare them and their children the pain of their migrations, it may help keep them the spirited and intelligent people they are.

Minnesota Cities, Towns, and Villages

By 1913, the year when 50 municipalities founded the League of Minnesota Cities, Minnesota had taken form. The Twin Cities, Minneapolis and St. Paul, had established themselves as the center of a commercial and industrial empire. With the exception of Rochester, by 1913 the primary regional service centers of Minnesota had emerged. They were Winona, Mankato, Moorhead, St. Cloud, Bemidji, and, the largest of all, Duluth, an international port that commanded the iron frontier.

In 1913 Minnesota's farm villages flourished. They had survived the farm depression of the 1890s. Farm prices were good. Their two- and three-block downtowns approximated the range of amenities of an improving world. Their main streets had general stores, bakeries, creameries, tractor and machinery dealers, and furniture dealers, who had enough lumber and means to haul things to double as undertakers. Most main streets also boasted a doctor, a lawyer, a school, a newspaper, a hotel, a library, and even an "opera house." The benefits of America were in Minnesota villages and towns.

When I arrived in southwest Minnesota in 1969 to teach at Southwest State, there were still signs of the vitality these villages once had. Many still had functioning main streets that offered a doctor, a dentist, a cinema, and, perhaps, a couple restaurants, to separate the sheep from the goats.

Each town seemed different. Each, with its row of elevators, church steeples, and water tower, left a different imprint on the horizon. Each village had its own ethnicity: Hendricks and Cottonwood were Norwegian, there were Danes in Tyler, Germans in Sanborn, Belgians in Ghent, Dutch in Edgerton, Icelanders in Minneota.

Each village seemed to have a different moral character. This village was gregarious, that one suspicious; this one was quarrelsome, while that one appeared to be held together by the work of a few. This village never entirely succeeded in integrating its English-named downtowners and the surrounding foreign-born farmers; while that one appeared, at least superficially, to be homogeneous from top to bottom.

The prosperity of the 1970s did not cover all signs of decline in the region. Although the population did not significantly decrease, the old increasingly outnumbered the young, farms were larger, farmers were fewer and older, and the most ambitious and best educated youth left the region for a better life elsewhere.

Thanks to automobiles and better roads, villagers and farmers drove to other towns and cities to work, shop, visit their doctor, get their public assistance, see a movie, or even to eat a meal. Stores along main street closed as customers became fewer in number and more varied in taste. The towns and villages of southwestern Minnesota were not the thriving entities they had been on the eve of the First World War. Railroad lines (the founding mechanism of the region) were abandoned in unprecedented numbers during the 1960s and 1970s.

From the farm crisis of the 1980s rural Minnesota appeared inescapably subjected to one unforgiving law . . . the more rural the county, the more certain its decline. (What had been spared southwest Minnesota in the 1970s was now suffered two-fold in the 1980s; that is, while it lost approximately one percent per year of population in the 1950s and 1960s, in the 1980s it lost two percent per year for having held its own in the 1970s.)

From the perspective of the crisis, the history of the villages and cities of southwest Minnesota took on increasing importance. Cities that had a population of 500 or less in 1920 barely held their own until 1950 and declined thereafter. Those that had 1,000 people in 1920 held their own until 1950, and were likely to decline thereafter. Those that had a population of about 2,000 in 1920 doubled by the 1950s, but thereafter had to struggle to maintain their size.

In retrospect, it now appears that size and date of incorporation were the primary determinants of future growth in rural Minnesota. That is, if a village was born late, it was born small, and if it was born small, it was not likely to prosper. (Or to state the converse, the sooner a site area was established the more likely it had a larger service area, received the benefits from being such a service center, and, therefore, grew and prospered.)

Three of the four counties which have not suffered a decline of population in southwest Minnesota have county seats that received significant public investment in the 1960s. Worthington, in Nobles County, and Willmar, in Kandiyohi County, were given community colleges, while Marshall, in Lyon County, got a state university.

These three cities alone have defied the overall trend of the area. They not only doubled in size between 1920 and 1950, but they went on to redouble again in the 1960s and 1970s while their equals struggled to stay the same. This is not to claim that public investment alone accounts for the success of these cities, however, nor does it assert that public investment alone (however large) can overcome the loss of a regional industry, as Duluth can testify. Nor does the present growth of Willmar, Worthington, and Marshall prove that these towns are necessarily sustaining growth. Indeed, one pressing question for southwest Minnesota is how will these three towns fare as their service regions decline and yet, as lead cities, they are forced to continue to supply the sophisticated goods, services, and amenities of an advancing civilization.

The farm crisis of the 1980s did not just alter my view of the present, but it also reinterpreted Minnesota's history for me. Minnesota is terribly young. There is nothing old about it. It is hardly older than my grandfather.

Minnesota was one of many new territories opened in the second half of the nineteenth century, when railroads initiated a new era of commerce and industry. Villages and towns were born on the drafting boards of railroad companies. They were located, named, put on a fixed grid, and given standard street names before their first inhabitants appeared.

Prairie towns were railroad builders' dreams. They were built by railroad founders' visions of great profits and thriving cities on the prairie supplying food to the gigantic new industrial cities. Minnesota railroad cities did not arise out of the natural and immediate flow of peoples and goods.

From the beginning many prairie railroad towns, especially along secondary railroad lines, were overbuilt. Some villages began to die the day they were born. From the day the towns were born, they began to compete. The number of possible settlers to attract was fixed (by size of farm and amount of surrounding land). One town's gain was another town's loss.

In the crisis of the 1980s the people of southwest Minnesota faced painful questions. Despite the richness of the soil and the nation's need for cheap food, is the agriculture of southwestern Minnesota—like Minnesota's lumber and mining—on the verge of being yet another failed frontier? In less than 100 years had the region run its course? Will the fate of the region's farmers and townspeople be any different than the sheepherders of the Scottish highlands, the shipbuilders of Glasgow, the coal miners of Pennsylvania, the fishermen of the Great Lakes, the factory workers of Detroit, or the iron miners of the Range?

With the crisis over but not forgotten, unpleasant certainties about the days ahead appear. Rural Minnesota will fall further and further behind its metropolitan neighbors. City and country cousins will know and understand each other less and less.

As the growing metropolitan areas are increasingly populated and led by people whose background is neither Minnesotan nor rural, the countryside itself will be populated on one hand by poorer people who need public assistance, and newly arrived outsiders on the other. Furthermore, the lead cities of the countryside, themselves inhabited by more and more outsiders, will be forced to try to find ways to cooperate with each other, despite having been conditioned to compete.

Two different Minnesotas will emerge. One will be a metropolitan Minnesota, running up the old Highway 52 from Rochester, through the Twin Cities to St. Cloud. This will be Minnesota's fertile crescent, where the population and the amenities are. It will be young and cosmopolitan, keep pace with the advancing civilization, and form the political majority of the state.

The other Minnesota will look through the window at its prospering neighbor. This Minnesota will struggle to keep up. It will be forced to learn cooperation when survival, throughout its history, has required competition. With a smaller tax base, it will have an increasingly difficult time staying even. With less and less, this second Minnesota must find a way to do more and more.

The challenge of Minnesota's future will involve avoiding a state composed of two contending groups of strangers: one engrossed in a world of expanding opportunities, the other preoccupied with the consequences of irretrievably failed frontiers.

To respond to this dilemma, some will speak of the need to disperse state government agencies across the state. Others, equally predictably, will propose a new, elaborate highway system to link rural and metropolitan Minnesota. Still others, dedicated to economic development, will seek by other means—such as the Greater Minnesota Corporation—to promote new industries in the regions of failed and failing frontiers.

Revealing my prejudice as a teacher, I consider education the state's best investment in its people. My argument is simple, and I believe it useful regardless of what the future holds for rural Minnesota. If rural society is to prosper, it must have a good educational system to attract and retain qualified people, companies, and leaders. If, however, rural society declines, as now appears likely, then both self-interest and fairness dictate that rural citizens receive a good education to equip its youth and adults for their eventual migration.

Unlike their migrant grandparents, today's migrants do not arrive to a new and open land. Frontiers of opportunity for the uneducated no longer exist. Ambition, determination, and luck no longer suffice. Today's migrants must go from one settled world to another.

CHAPTER ONE

More of the Same, More with Less

For Minnesota and its leaders, the twenty-first century will be more of the same; it will be more with less. By virtue of belonging to an advancing and specializing civilization moved by more and more wants, laws, and functions; leaders, especially rural leaders, will increasingly find themselves trying to do more with less. The issue has been, and will continue to be, keeping up.

The year 2000 will be a millenarian year but not a magical year. What comes after it will be a rough copy of the two decades that went before it. The demographics of Minnesota's future are found in its past trends. With some exceptions, these trends can be stated as laws that predict the future. The first law is, "Where there has been growth in the last decades, there will be more growth in the following decades." The second law, as suggested by Graph One (pp. 26), is, "Where regions and towns have diminished, they will further diminish."

Having started to build a world out of laws, postulates and conjectures follow. The first postulate—the more rural the county and the area, the more likely its decline. Major exceptions to this postulate are created by unusual natural amenities (nothing like a few trees, a lake, and a highway or two to excite visions of the good life), and the proximity of a thriving regional center, whose economic growth, and educational, medical, and recreational amenities make for good suburban living.

THE DECLINE OF RURAL MINNESOTA

A second postulate suggests that the smaller the town, the more likely its decline. Smaller towns suffer continual out-migration of people seeking to obtain better jobs and careers and more amenities, and to escape unemployment, underemployment, eroding incomes, and poverty, all of which increasingly pervade the

GRAPH ONE:

Population Trends of Selected Cities in Minnesota

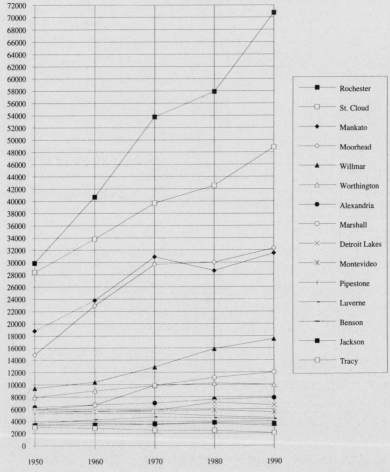

rural regions of the state.

A third postulate is that the primary determinant of the size of cities, towns, and villages is the date of settlement and magnitude at time of incorporation. That is, if a village was born late, it was born small, and so it tended to stay. Conversely, a larger

GRAPH TWO:
*Population Trends of Selected Cities
with Populations Below 1,000 in 1950*

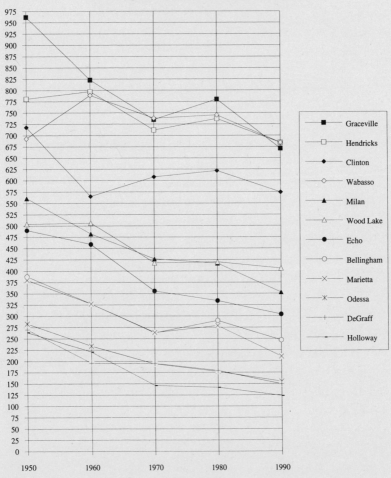

town is an older town. Most larger towns were founded along important crossroads (even a key waterway), and had, right from the outset, more private capital and public investment supporting their quest for regional dominance. Early Italian physicist Evangelista Torricelli's law of cannon balls can roughly serve to describe and predict the path of the demographic history of Minnesota's cities. The more recently the village was shot off, the smaller its arc, the lower its trajectory, the sooner, and more certain, its return to earth. In slightly less academic terms, the smaller towns (launched with fewer numbers, less capital, and a smaller mission) rather quickly reached their maximum height before beginning their gradual descent.

Different arcs describe the flights of different-sized towns. Once the factors of natural amenities and the proximity to metropolitan or regional centers are discounted, the growth of Minnesota cities is fairly predictable. As is illustrated in Graph Two (pp. 27), villages of 250 to 300 inhabitants clearly began their descent two, three, and four decades ago; towns of 300 to 1,000 inhabitants have likewise entered patterns of decline over the last two or three decades, unless located in the proximity of a regional center or in a resort area. Pessimistically, it is even possible to argue that towns in rural areas of 1,000 or more that almost doubled their populations in the period from 1930 to 1970 have now leveled off and are entering their downward arc. Declines of some towns of the size of 5,000 and even 10,000 have particularly ominous implications for many areas of the countryside.

Evidence from southwestern Minnesota supports the pessimistic view of the future of Minnesota's rural order, as forecast by the state demographer in his April 1991 *News and Notes*. He confirmed that, while Minnesota was the fastest growing state in the Midwest, the growth of the 1980s was slower than the 1970s and, with few exceptions, significant growth was confined to metropolitan Minnesota, Minnesota's new and emerging "fertile crescent" which runs up old Highway 52 from Rochester through the Twin Cities to St. Cloud. Over 55 percent of the state's population now resides in the ten-county Twin Cities metropolitan area. Elsewhere, again exempting places where natural amenities or a regional center commanded, losses were keen.

More than the population numbers from the 1990 census confirm the overall pessimistic predictions for rural Minnesota. Rural regions around the world are in decline. Throughout the rural world factors favoring migration prove stronger than governmental planning and philanthropic intention, while notions of rural development, for a variety of reasons, prove far weaker than major historical trends.

Other things within the nation at large argue for more of the same ahead. Rural populations are older and thus more likely to die. In the countryside, especially after the disastrous 1980s, wages are down and underemployment and poverty are up. Farms are larger and farm families are smaller. Less and less capital finds its way into rural villages and smaller rural towns.

Rural areas, increasingly poorer and older, are losing their tax base. Their professionals, starting with doctors and going down the line, are paid less for their work. Only the most naïve count a non-unionized and underemployed labor force—willing to accept low wages, minimum job benefits, and the absence of job security—a bait worthy of catching good fish.

Beyond this, there are other negative factors, not easily calculable, that lead people to leave rural regions. It is increasingly apparent that to stay in a rural area is to elect to remain poor and, thus, to lack the means to live a full life, which we moderns cherish more than anything else. There are those persistent, nagging feelings that to remain in the countryside is to spend one's life treading time in the backwater of history.

There are other important factors for migration that we can more easily calculate. These factors play on different age groups with different power. They constitute what demographers call age-specific migration. For the young in rural areas, there are fewer good jobs and educational opportunities are distant. For those in their mid-twenties there are no real or long-standing career opportunities in the private sector. For those in their late twenties and thirties there is the dawning awareness that one's initiatives and speculations, from starting up stores to perfecting new agricultural technologies, are marked by failure; that one's children won't get all the benefits they could in larger towns and school systems; and finally, for those approaching retirement, health care, care of the elderly, and other amenities that the aging want in greater and greater amounts are more likely to be found in a regional center than in a village or town.

In the simplest terms, rural people's wants and needs (which are not easily distinguished from one another) lead them from the smaller villages to larger towns and cities. Regional centers (still relatively free of violence, drugs, disorder, and social chaos) inevitably gain at the expense of smaller villages and towns, but even they can lose populations as people jump them to shop, to get services, and to live in larger regional centers whose job and educational opportunities and amenities make them irrefutably more attractive.

Again southwestern Minnesota can be used to illustrate this process. Of the nineteen southwestern counties, only a single county, Kandiyohi, emerged from the disastrous 1980s without a loss. Its growth was entirely dependent on its lead city, Willmar, thanks to Willmar's roles as railroad center, regional service and political center, regional medical center (which is especially big business in the land of the aging), and a long history of public investment that provided Willmar with a community college, technical college, and a state hospital.

Declines in the 1980s reaching twenty percent occurred along the southern, western, and northern borders of the state. In the

1990s, declines in the most rural areas should return to rates of loss that typified the 1960s and 1970s. The population in these areas will be older. The smaller cities and towns, both comparatively and absolutely, will experience a loss of amenities (schools above all else).

In the 1980s, the more rural a county was, the greater the likelihood of its decline; the smaller the town, the more likely it lost people to near and distant centers. Only strong rural regional centers themselves were able to counterbalance the population loss of their respective counties as they struggled to escape the rural decline that encircled them. In the 1990s, regional centers will have to expand their efforts to offer meaningful job and career opportunities, as well as establish a full horizon of amenities for themselves and their service areas.

The smaller towns and cities will find it more and more difficult to keep up with the advancing world around them. Once each village had its own character, often its own ethnic identity, and formed in some degree a social and political community. With its doctor, dentist, lawyer, bowling alley, movie theater, hardware store, hotel, café, and town schools and baseball teams, it had about what any good Twin Cities neighborhood would have. Now, the small towns and cities, and even some regional centers, are falling further and further behind, as stores and downtowns are closed and people increasingly find their entertainment, goods, and opportunities for a full life elsewhere.

Even their long-standing claim to having amenities comparable to their urban neighborhoods becomes dubious. While free of the crime of the big cities, they must risk having inferior medical treatment. Although once they clearly provided a community and an identity, increasingly threats against community are heard amid talk of closing and pairing schools, all the people who went away, the end of the town's newspaper, and the strangers who fill the town's trailer courts. They talk about the need for their children to migrate and the good sense their aging parent showed by moving down the road, if not to the Sunbelt, where there is more for the old to do and better medical treatment.

There is simply no way for taxes or public investment to reverse (at least consistently and permanently) the flow to thriving and amenity-filled metropolitan centers from distant rural areas of Minnesota, no matter how great the attraction of knowing the world one lives in. As people learn of a better world, they are less likely to deny themselves and their children the amenities of job advancement, health, educational opportunity, and excitement.

Significant numbers of new immigrants will not come to the most rural areas of Minnesota, and there is no reason to assume that the metropolitan center, however powerful, will continue to sink its precious money, limited imagination and intelligence, and exhaustible energy in its rural periphery. There is a limit to all things.

Without embracing the most cynical position—that the metropolitan area can do no intended good for rural areas—there is a question as to how much it can help. The concept of rural development itself has little precise value. Surely rural areas cannot expect state government, inspired by philanthropy or driven by free enterprise, to bring prosperity, order, or even stability to the countryside. After all, if world history is a guide to Minnesota experience, peripheries serve rather than are served by metropolitan centers.

The proposition that rural areas must take care of rural areas is probably meaningless, if it implies anything more than the exchange of votes on certain issues in the legislature. This would imply cooperation and leadership that is without precedent in the state.

Leaving aside Minnesota's iron range, where unique forms of political cooperation and uses of political influence (derived from union and ethnic traditions) have flourished, there can be little hope that rural areas will learn to cooperate in the 1990s. Necessity itself does not create community; at least it certainly hasn't so far in southwestern Minnesota. Pessimism about the promise of rural and intraregional cooperation exists for two other reasons.

First, the villages, towns, and cities of the rural area are historically conditioned to competition, not cooperation. While professing the mutual advancement of town, business, and civilization, civic boosterism, the most energetic philosophy of the American city, has always been competitive rather than cooperative. Boosterism, whose lessons have been supported by experience, has repeatedly taught a winner-take-all attitude. The city that gets an industry, a college, or other significant private or public investments, goes on to grow and thrive, while the loser falls permanently behind.

In part, pessimism about rural Minnesota comes from a negative assessment about the promise of rural cooperation on a regional and a state level. It also arises from the absence of rural leadership, especially in regional centers, where the fate of rural Minnesota hinges.

Perhaps it is true that the best rural leaders are gone, having left rural Minnesota. Even if this is not true, rural leaders, mirroring the area they represent, invariably become fewer, get older, and are asked to account for themselves in the face of an ever more complicated world. For rural leaders, there are more wants, more needs, more laws, more things to be mastered.

Rural leaders have lost more and more power to a distant world, and they are less and less able to define their local worlds. Increasingly, they face the burgeoning demands of their own diversifying populations for greater amenities, and the mounting requirements of a centralizing state and its imperious agents. All this tempts rural leaders to surrender in an attitude of resignation.

THE DECLINE OF RURAL MINNESOTA

Paralyzing rural leaders' thoughts and actions are two irreconcilable imperatives: More amenities! Less taxes! Amenities attract, taxes repel. Paradoxically, leaders are expected to raise more money to make their communities more attractive, but are also expected to keep taxes low to make their towns attractive. Raising taxes is doubly difficult where average incomes are significantly below state averages and below national poverty levels, as they are in the most rural areas of Minnesota.

Rural leaders are contradictorily asked to secure the first good of civilization, an improved quality of life, while creating new jobs, the most essential thing of all for rural survival. The generation of jobs, however, is frequently formulated with strategies predicated on lower taxes, lower wages, and an underemployed labor force, none of which make for a better communal life in either the short- or long-term.

These divided views, eluding clear analysis and confounding public policy, will continue to play themselves out in rural areas. They will continue to cause confusion and discouragement over public policy, while fueling a growing sense of resignation.

Rural leaders, however, rarely despair. At times many still dream of that prince who, just around the corner, will soon appear to fit his slipper of economic prosperity on the city's fair foot and lead her away to higher levels of civilization. But these days more and more rural leaders are more and more likely than in the recent past to understand that this dream is just that, a dream. Older, wiser, they are more likely to go about the important business of running their cities with far less grandiose visions and dreams than their predecessors.

Leadership from state government cannot be expected to save the countryside. Governor and legislators alike lack a vision of Minnesota's future and are as helpless as the state's rural leaders.

In time only law and self-interest will form the sinew of Minnesota. Metropolitan Minnesota will be younger, richer, better educated, and filled with more people who, by background, tradition, and interest, will have less and less understanding of and sympathy for the continual and costly demands of rural Minnesota. The world of rural Minnesota will increasingly appear to be a burden, possessing fewer and fewer redeeming qualities.

This view assumes that the challenge of keeping up with the amenities of an advancing civilization belongs exclusively to rural regions and their lead cities, when in fact this test belongs to the entire state and the whole nation. As civilization advances, it demands more specialization, it defines a higher level of common and expected good, and further expands and differentiates people's desires for a full life. All this makes civilization more costly in people and money, and shows how the very desires that make a civilization can also destroy a civilization.

People want things, the old as well as the young, and the more they get, the more they want. They don't just want basic things like clean water, a good sewage system, houses, cars and good roads to run them on. But they long for a lot more, including expensive tennis shoes, fancy vacations, and even income tax-free states. Their wishes, which include decent jobs, a good education, interesting careers, diverse opportunities, and good health care, turn eventually into expectations and are presumed to be natural and right. Expectations tend to outrun satisfactions; for every good supplied, two new wants arise. This means there will be greater demands on public and private sectors to supply the good life, and want will invariably outrun local resources.

Multiplying wants sire multiplying complexity. New technologies, new laws, and new social groups create forests of conflicting interests and conflicting bureaucracies.

Metropolitan centers, which increasingly are forced to take

up Washington's work, must struggle as hard as rural areas to try to keep up with advancing civilization. With their cores thrown into jeopardy by crime, drugs, social disorder, and the flight of middle-class taxpayers to surrounding suburbs, it is not easy to fashion political coalitions and meet the growing horizon of rights, wants, and necessities. If not to fall further behind and eventually go the way of many great cities of this nation, metropolitan leaders must not only supply jobs, careers, benefits and amenities, but social peace, order, and tranquillity. Minnesota's state leaders, like their cousins both in Washington, D.C., and rural Minnesota, do not escape the fatiguing pressures of keeping up with a developing civilization and, thus, doing more with less.

This chapter concludes almost as abruptly as it began. Expect no millennium in the year 2000. Expect more of the same, expect to do more with less, as Minnesotans, rural and metropolitan alike, have to try to keep pace with a world in which complexity and immensity of want outpace their communities, their leadership, their ability to cooperate, and just possibly, their resources of money and intelligence. Just keeping up will amount to running the good race, a race far better than that being run in Washington between the United States and the changing world.

Metropolitan centers must struggle to offer safety and security, for without them, their amenities will not suffice. They will only attract commuters and visitors. More and more, those left in the centers (who aren't very taxable) will come to feel that they are prisoners of a hopeless situation.

If Minnesotans must choose where public and private money is to go in rural areas, it is best to direct investment to regional lead cities. Supply them with the fullest range of amenities possible, for they alone can stave off sharp decline and minimize the distance between life in the countryside and the city. In turn, integrate them as fully as possible into the life of the cities.

Finally, on the matter of education, accept migration as a reality and prepare our citizens as best we can for the longest possible migration, a migration that may for some rival in distance, complexity, and anguish those long journeys made by their immigrant grandparents and great-grandparents.

Education does not end migration; education encourages it. While enhancing people's humanity and teaching people to appreciate and understand their inheritance, it also instructs them that all are migrants in the modern world.

From every point of view, including public cost, it is better that people, especially poor and rural people, migrate by their wishes, potential, and skills rather than remain sedentary because of poverty, ignorance, and despair. If those educated in the countryside stay in the countryside, all the better: they and their talents are needed. If they leave, Godspeed! They have been prepared, made worthy of a civilization that makes migration toward the better life, as illusory as this can be, its highest good.

CHAPTER TWO

Natural Decline
in Rural Minnesota

A theory of decline underlies this book. The smaller the town, the more likely its decline; and the more rural the county, the more likely its decline. To add worse news to bad news, natural decline has begun in rural Minnesota.

As Table One (pp. 40–41) demonstrates, natural decline appears in those parts of rural Minnesota where out-migration has been greatest, where the population loss has been strongest, and where the population has grown oldest.

Natural decline—the condition in which, during a given period, deaths exceed births—surfaced in the 1980s in rural Minnesota. In the first five years of the decade, it appeared in only two counties, Norman and Aitkin. In the second five years of the decade, however, it appeared in twelve counties (see Table Two, pp. 42, and Map One, pp. 43). Nine of the counties were in southwestern Minnesota, two in northwestern Minnesota, and one in north central Minnesota. Three consequences associated with natural decline are the loss of population, the aging of the population, and accompanying breakdown of civic leadership.

Natural decline compounded the rates of decline in rural areas in the second half of this century because of lower childbirth rates, emigration, and a shrinking and aging farm population. It will contribute to the acceleration of population losses that have

THE DECLINE OF RURAL MINNESOTA

TABLE ONE:

Patterns of Natural Change, Population Change, and Median Age for Counties in Rural Minnesota

The three ranks for percent natural change, percent population change, and percent migration are presented regressively. The higher the rank for the percent of natural change, the more the number of deaths exceeds the number of births. (Counties experiencing more deaths than births are represented as negative percentages.) The higher the rank for the percent of population change, the greater the population loss. (Counties experiencing population decline are represented as negative percentages.) The higher the rank for percent of migration, the greater the out-migration. (Negative percentages indicate out-migration.) The fourth rank for median age is presented progressively, that is, the higher the rank for median age, the greater the median age.

County	Percent Natural Change 1980–1990	Rank	Percent Pop. Change 1980–1990	Rank	Percent Migration 1980–1990	Rank	Median Age 1990	Rank
Norman	-1.42	71	-14.97	62	-13.55	51	39	63
Aitkin	-0.69	70	-7.3	42	-6.61	25	42.8	71
Grant	0.14	69	-12.9	55	-13.04	48	40.7	68
Big Stone	0.45	68	-18.55	69	-19	67	40.4	67
Lincoln	0.49	67	-16.05	66	-16.53	60	41.4	70
Kittson	0.96	66	-13.56	57	-14.52	55	38.6	60
Lac Qui Parle	1	65	-15.75	64	-16.75	61	39.4	66
Cottonwood	1.08	64	-14.54	60	-15.62	56	39.2	64
Traverse	1.14	63	-19.47	70	-20.61	69	41.3	69
Pope	1.48	62	-7.82	45	-9.31	34	38.5	59
Swift	1.52	61	-17	67	-18.51	65	38	56
Faribault	1.71	60	-14.09	58	-15.8	57	38.9	62
Yellow Medicine	1.96	59	-14.42	59	-16.38	59	37.6	54
Pipestone	2.62	58	-10.26	50	-12.87	47	36	41
Cass	2.66	57	3.52	16	0.86	7	38.3	57
Fillmore	2.66	56	6.06	10	-7.92	29	36.4	42
Chippewa	2.88	55	-11.47	53	-14.35	54	37.5	53
Otter Tail	2.97	54	-2.35	30	-5.32	23	37.3	51
Koochiching	2.98	53	-7.24	41	-10.22	37	35.6	35
Wadena	3.06	52	-7.31	43	-10.37	38	36	40
Lake	3.07	51	-20.15	71	-23.22	71	39.2	65
Mower	3.08	50	-7.44	44	-10.52	39	37.4	52
Cook	3.1	49	-5.47	34	-8.58	30	38.3	58
Marshall	3.11	48	-15.61	63	-18.72	66	36.5	44
Freeborn	3.32	47	-9	49	-12.32	45	37.1	50
Redwood	3.33	46	-10.79	51	-14.12	53	36.7	46
Martin	3.42	45	-7.18	40	-10.6	40	37	49
Renville	3.45	44	-13.37	56	-16.82	62	36.7	47
Murray	3.75	43	-16.05	65	-19.81	68	38.8	61

Natural Decline in Rural Minnesota

County	Percent Natural Change 1980–1990	Rank	Percent Pop. Change 1980–1990	Rank	Percent Migration 1980–1990	Rank	Median Age 1990	Rank
Jackson	3.8	42	-14.7	61	-18.5	64	36.9	48
Clearwater	3.81	41	-5.16	33	-8.97	33	36.5	43
Watonwan	3.91	40	-5.49	35	-9.4	35	35.7	36
Stevens	4.02	39	-6.08	37	-10.1	36	30.5	6
Pennington	4.08	38	-12.79	54	-16.87	63	34.1	18
Hubbard	4.43	37	5.97	11	1.54	4	37.7	55
Mille Lacs	4.62	36	1.3	22	-3.32	16	34.8	26
Goodhue	4.66	35	5.01	14	0.35	9	34.2	19
Sibley	4.67	34	-7	39	-11.68	44	35.5	33
Carlton	4.69	33	-2.26	29	-6.95	27	34.9	28
Mahnomen	4.72	32	-8.87	48	-13.59	52	35	30
Red Lake	4.73	31	-17.29	68	-22.03	70	35.5	34
Nobles	4.76	30	-7.98	46	-12.73	46	35.8	38
Douglas	4.9	29	3	19	-1.9	13	35.2	31
Wilkin	4.94	28	-11.1	52	-16.04	58	34.4	22
Crow Wing	5	27	6.06	9	1.06	6	35.8	37
Rock	5.17	26	-8.38	47	-13.55	50	36.6	45
Pine	5.23	24	7.01	6	1.78	3	34.5	23
Lake of the Woods	5.23	25	8.29	4	3.06	2	35.5	32
Brown	5.33	23	-5.8	36	-11.13	42	34.5	24
Meeker	5.44	22	1.22	23	-4.22	20	34.9	27
Itasca	5.61	21	-5.12	32	-10.73	41	35.9	39
Houston	5.82	20	-0.63	25	-5.2	22	34.2	21
Wabasha	5.85	19	2.12	20	-3.73	18	34.2	20
Winona	5.99	18	3.4	17	-2.59	15	30.2	5
Le Sueur	6.23	17	-0.83	26	-7.07	28	33.5	17
Becker	6.34	16	-0.0496	31	-11.3	43	35	29
Todd	6.71	15	-6.51	38	-13.22	49	34.6	25
Kanabec	6.83	14	5.27	13	-1.56	12	33.5	16
Waseca	6.87	13	-2	28	-8.87	32	32.2	11
Rice	6.87	12	6.72	7	-0.15	10	30.2	4
Lyon	7.06	11	-1.66	27	-8.72	31	31.6	9
McLeod	7.19	10	8	5	0.81	8	32.9	14
Blue Earth	7.21	9	3.31	18	-3.9	19	27.6	1
Kandiyohi	7.49	8	5.43	12	-2.05	14	33	15
Morrison	7.85	7	1	24	-6.85	26	32.7	13
Steele	7.92	6	1.32	21	-6.6	24	32.7	12
Isanti	8.51	5	9.83	3	1.32	5	32	10
Roseau	8.78	4	19.5	1	10.72	1	30.6	7
Nicollet	8.92	3	4.26	15	-4.66	21	30.1	3
Dodge	9.89	2	6.48	8	-3.4	17	31.6	8
Beltrami	11.45	1	10.98	2	-0.58	11	29.2	2

THE DECLINE OF RURAL MINNESOTA

TABLE TWO:
Natural Change Between 1985–1990
for Rural Minnesota Counties

County	Natural Change 1985–1990	Rank	County	Natural Change 1985–1990	Rank
Aitkin	-154	71	Sibley	279	35
Norman	-139	70	Pine	335	34
Lincoln	-77	69	Kanabec	336	33
Swift	-64	68	Mille Lacs	337	32
Big Stone	-61	67	Nobles	367	31
Grant	-53	66	Mower	380	30
Kittson	-46	65	Freeborn	426	29
Traverse	-37	64	Wabasha	436	28
Cottonwood	-32	63	Meeker	439	27
Lac Qui Parle	-31	62	Carlton	473	26
Yellow Medicine	-9	61	Waseca	489	24
Pope	-3	60	Douglas	495	25
Red Lake	40	59	Houston	516	23
Cook	46	58	Otter Tail	523	22
Faribault	51	57	Brown	541	21
Lake	52	56	Le Sueur	546	20
Chippewa	61	55	Todd	583	19
Murray	65	54	Dodge	620	18
Mahnomen	77	53	Roseau	640	17
Marshall	89	52	Goodhue	675	16
Koochiching	94	51	Stevens	676	15
Lake of the Woods	105	50	Lyon	684	14
Pipestone	109	49	Itasca	721	13
Clearwater	121	48	Becker	757	12
Watonwon	121	47	Crow Wing	879	11
Jackson	141	46	Isanti	918	10
Wadena	142	45	Morrison	976	9
Renville	148	44	McLeod	1020	8
Martin	153	43	Steele	1053	7
Wilkin	166	42	Nicollet	1061	6
Rock	170	41	Kandiyohi	1223	5
Fillmore	174	40	Winona	1232	4
Cass	177	39	Rice	1445	3
Pennington	199	38	Blue Earth	1567	2
Redwood	232	37	Beltrami	1712	1
Hubbard	254	36			

MAP ONE:
Natural Change 1985–1990

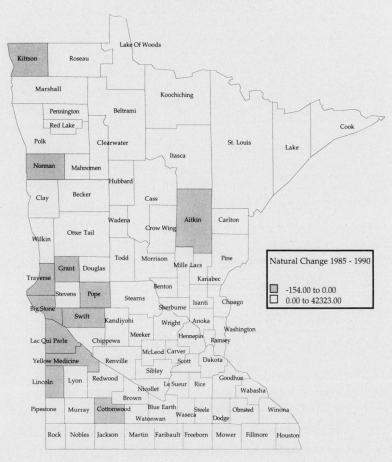

Lake Of Woods

Kittson · Roseau

Marshall · Koochiching

Pennington · Beltrami

Red Lake

Polk · Clearwater · St. Louis · Lake · Cook

Itasca

Norman · Mahnomen

Hubbard

Clay · Becker · Cass

Wadena · Aitkin · Carlton

Wilkin · Otter Tail · Crow Wing

Todd · Morrison · Pine

Grant · Douglas · Mille Lacs

Traverse · Kanabec

Stevens · Pope · Benton

Big Stone · Stearns · Isanti · Chisago

Swift · Sherburne

Kandiyohi · Anoka

Wright · Washington

Lac Qui Parle · Meeker · Hennepin · Ramsey

Chippewa · McLeod · Carver · Dakota

Yellow Medicine · Renville · Scott

Sibley · Goodhue

Lincoln · Lyon · Redwood · Le Sueur · Rice · Wabasha

Nicollet

Brown

Pipestone · Murray · Cottonwood · Blue Earth · Steele · Olmsted · Winona

Watonwan · Waseca · Dodge

Rock · Nobles · Jackson · Martin · Faribault · Freeborn · Mower · Fillmore · Houston

Natural Change 1985 - 1990

☐ -154.00 to 0.00
☐ 0.00 to 42323.00

43

characterized the small- and medium-size cities (5,000 population and below) in the 1970s and 1980s.

Population loss has—and will continue to have—serious consequences. Property will decline in value. Downtowns will die. Ever greater numbers of smaller cities (starting with the smallest and the youngest) will stand as mere skeletons of a former life.

The countryside itself, to use a favorite rural measure of vacancy, will be dotted by empty wells. A Redwood County commissioner recently estimated that his highly productive agricultural county has 3,000 empty wells.

Although there will be exceptions, more and more rural areas and cities will recognize that there are simply insufficient numbers of people to sustain their economy and institutions. Fewer farmers will come to town. More and more offices of mayor, council, and school board will be filled by write-in candidates. Rural Minnesota will experience the decline and perhaps the disincorporation common to much of the Dakotas since their settlement. Towns will be fewer, farms larger, and spaces emptier. The great settling of the prairie will reverse itself.

Before Regions Decline, They Age

No longer benefiting from significant capital investment and without meaningful work, rural youth emigrate. The area's brightest and most ambitious couples decide not to stay. The oldest, the least educated, and the poorest remain behind.

As throughout rural regions of the nation and the world, rural Minnesota is characterized by an aging population. Southwest Minnesota illustrates this. According to demographer Jerry Heil, between 1950 and 1970 the population of age 35 and over went from 42.5 percent to 47.4 percent; from 1970 to 1990, it went to 52.4 percent.

In the counties where natural decline is occurring, the population is aging. This is true of all the cities of these counties, except for the smallest. The median age has increased relatively consistently between 1970 and 1990 in those cities with populations from 5,000 to 2,500 people, cities with populations 2,500 to 1,000 people, and cities with 1,000 to 500 people (see Table Three, pp. 46–47). However, it has increased in only about half of the cities with populations of less than 500 people.

This observation regarding the smallest cities squares with the intuition that any given population can only get so old before it vanishes or gets younger. It also accords with the fact that in the smallest cities when the old die, there are few middle-aged people to replace them, since they migrated long ago. Also, a comparative absence of nursing homes and amenities in the smallest villages contributes to the exodus of the old and the decrease of median age.

No sign of the overall aging of rural Minnesota cities is as telling as the closing of a school and the opening of a nursing home. With hospitals closing and doctors vanishing, rural cities have begun to ask whether they have the means to satisfy those growing old, who each year are older and more diversified and, correspondingly, have greater wants and needs.

Can Politics Remain Viable?

Another set of questions associated with the aging of rural Minnesota turns on the issue of the continuing viability of civic politics in rural Minnesota. In play are such additional questions as who exactly the rural old are and what their growing presence means for rural politics. Unfortunately, these questions remain unstudied and leave the field wide open to conjectures.

First, differentiating the old into three groups—the young old, the middle old, and the old old—the young and the middle old will probably continue to vote or not vote more or less as they always have. By definition itself, the old old are going to vote less because of increasing physical or mental impairment.

THE DECLINE OF RURAL MINNESOTA

Change in Median Age Between 1970–1990
for Cities Located in Counties that Experienced
Natural Decline Between 1985–1990

	Population 1990	Median Age 1970	Median Age 1990
Population 5,000–2,501			
Windom	4283	31.80	38.10
Benson	3235	38.00	40.80
Granite Falls	3083	30.00	38.10
Glenwood	2573	42.30	44.20
Population 2,500–1,001			
Ortonville	2205	36.80	44.00
Madison	1951	44.40	51.10
Mountain Lake	1906	43.60	46.30
Canby	1826	41.80	46.60
Wheaton	1651	42.20	48.00
Dawson	1626	44.90	44.30
Appleton	1552	46.10	45.80
Tyler	1257	50.50	45.00
Elbow Lake	1186	37.10	41.50
Starbuck	1143	50.00	54.50
Clarkfield	1003	42.50	39.00
Population 1,000-501			
Westbrook	853	43.20	54.40
Browns Valley	804	40.90	44.70
Ivanhoe	751	43.50	44.10
Kerkhoven	732	35.10	38.30
Lake Benton	693	39.80	51.60
Hendricks	684	50.10	64.70
Graceville	671	36.60	43.50
Hoffman	576	43.20	45.90
Clinton	574	48.20	47.70

Natural Decline in Rural Minnesota

	Population 1990	Median Age 1970	Median Age 1990
Population 500 and Under			
Herman	485	39.90	40.60
Jeffers	443	46.70	38.60
Wood Lake	406	45.40	33.90
Ashby	350	49.50	51.20
Barrett	350	56.20	58.80
Cyrus	328	45.20	37.60
Echo	304	48.90	39.50
Storden	283	38.90	42.50
Murdock	282	34.40	38.20
Boyd	251	43.50	36.30
Bellingham	247	36.90	40.10
Villard	247	38.40	34.90
Hanley Falls	246	48.90	35.30
Lowry	233	38.80	41.70
Marietta	211	41.50	44.00
Porter	210	42.00	34.20
Long Beach	204	38.90	41.10
Clontarf	172	34.70	30.30
Wendell	159	34.80	48.90
Odessa	155	36.30	34.70
DeGraff	149	29.50	35.30
Dumont	126	29.50	38.30
Holloway	123	41.00	40.40
St. Leo	111	38.00	53.40
Arco	104	50.90	40.00
Norcross	98	46.90	38.80
Nassau	83	47.80	35.80
Hazel Run	81	30.80	35.80
Farwell	74	30.60	35.70
Tintah	74	34.20	38.30
Sedan	63	56.30	29.50
Westport	47	20.60	28.10
Louisburg	42	51.10	50.00

In a study of senior citizens in Florida published in *Gerontologist* (1989), Walter Rosenbaum and Jane Button argue that those who want new programs and more spending should not see seniors as objects of political fear. As of now, the old in Florida have not assembled themselves into a "gray peril," a single voting block or active coalition to oppose taxes for community growth, the provision of services, and benefits for other population groups. Nevertheless, the truth of Florida today may not prove to be the truth of Minnesota either today or tomorrow, for the old of the Snowbelt are not the old of the Sunbelt. In contrast to their richer, more mobile, and better-educated cousins in the sun, the old of the Snowbelt are, in far greater numbers, likely to live on modest and fixed incomes. For them, increased taxes constitute a threat to their standard of living and to their homes, which are their primary asset.

Minnesota's stay-at-home rural old might be transformed into a voting block consistently voting against tax increases. They have long been exposed to the anti-union and anti-big government teaching and preaching of local business leaders, the tight-fisted practices of county commissioners, and (like the rest of the nation during the last decade) strong anti-taxation rhetoric.

If Minnesota's rural old begin to vote as a block, their interest will be to pay less for public amenities, even if these amenities are essential to retain or to attract the middle-class couples with children who alone represent future vitality for their communities. The matter of school bond votes is particularly at issue.

Beyond the question of voting, there is the issue of the political participation of the old. In growing numbers the old are not natives of the cities where they reside. They often have followed retirement from work or farm with a migration, usually short, out of their immediate locale to a village or city in the region. Hence they are not conditioned by a long-standing civic pride to be concerned about the long-term well being of their newly adopted cities, even though the interests of their children and grandchildren might shape their voting.

Anecdotal information underlines another facet of declining local political participation. In the small cities during the past few decades, there seems to have been an exodus of those who traditionally lead. Often feeling unappreciated, exhausted, or simply ready to get on to something else, they have withdrawn from their roles as local leaders.

Leadership for them meant the constant burden of doing more with less. They faced the growing complexities of state government and its agencies, mounting local divisions, and fellow citizens increasingly willing to punish the business of an errant official by shopping in other communities. After decades of having held a wide range of leadership positions, the traditional leaders in small cities are concluding the game isn't worth the candle.

Now, as in preceding decades, the old guard in rural Minnesota (who represented the business and building class of cities) are stepping down. With them goes a tradition of leadership and a political community that prided itself on keeping up with its neighbor cities and the nation itself. Quietly, but just as certainly, the generations of new leaders are abandoning the guiding notion that their city is an integral part of an advancing civilization and at the cutting edge of history.

Although this notion was always more pretense than reality, it gave small cities a kind of dignity and a spiritual momentum even as the world that founded them was fast leaving them behind. Increasingly, the children and grandchildren of early business founders haul down the flag of civic boosterism and pursue the more modest goal of surviving as best they can. The leaders of smaller cities now boast that they still have a bank, an elevator, a post office, and a grocery store.

What's Ahead?

Natural decline has appeared in rural Minnesota. The young are gone and the old are hanging on. The prairie is no longer a magnet for distant capital. Tracks have been ripped up; downtowns are coming undone; amenities—like school, recreation, and medicine—vanish; populations don't coalesce; leaders do not cohere. The initiative of civilization has been lost. The idea of a new commercial order on the prairie fades. It recedes toward the east from whence it came.

A new rural order lies ahead. It will be smaller, weaker, and more subordinated to the policies, complexities, technicalities, and contradictions of its metropolitan center. This order, if it is to survive, will have to use its old to lead and to care for its old. It will have to develop a new vision of leadership. In this order the business community will no longer dominate; farmers will be fewer; disincorporation of towns will become common; policies and amenities will have to be implemented regionally. Local governments will be run by mixtures of those who are left behind and those who are new to the locale.

Although we do not know the future, we expect that the gods take more pleasure in change than most people do. Perhaps they might even enjoy making two authors dead wrong. We hope so. Nevertheless, for the moment, natural decline has raised its hoary head on the rural horizon.

CHAPTER THREE

If the Home Team Doesn't Win

The devastating 1980s, marked by the farm crisis, followed by the nationally depressed economy of the early 1990s, has accelerated the depopulation and aging of Minnesota's most rural towns and counties, and the long-term decline of its rural cities as civic and commercial entities. Rural Minnesota's main industry, agriculture, supports fewer and fewer families on the land. Its smaller cities no longer supply the things and the services its people need and want. Its institutions and professionals strain to keep up with the commands, the goods, and the increasing specialization of the outside world. The most severe pessimists look to the west to predict what lies ahead. "As went South Dakota, so go we." They tell proud and progressive Minnesotans that they should learn to live with decline gracefully.

Whether or not one agrees, few will dispute that the region is witnessing the breakdown of the compact established with the founding of its communities. In concert with the great bravado of railroads, entrepreneurs, and land speculators, the founders of its cities promised a "middle ground" between the nation's expanding industrial cities and the new farmers of the prairie. They assumed that they would offer the best things and embody the best that American civilization had to offer.

From the start, the enormous and accelerating growth of goods and services of the metropolitan center made light of the promises even of larger rural cities to keep up. Economic events exposed small towns and merchants as helpless, ambivalent spectators during serious crises when protesting farmers squared off against distant metropolises.

The 1890s were one such period. Afflicted by drought, disastrously low farm prices, and high railroad rates, many farmers organized themselves in the Populist party and attacked monopolies and the control of distant powers.

The poor farm economy of the 1920s and the depressed national economy of the 1930s also put small cities' promises to represent and embody advancing American civilization in abeyance. No different than the farmers—whose ranks were filled with sharecroppers—small-town merchants hunkered down and tried to survive. Not surprisingly, city services decreased; even leisure activities themselves ended, as golf courses and race tracks were plowed up and city baseball teams were abandoned. (These same forces put an end to girls' teams and sports in schools.) The League of Minnesota Cities turned its attention away from progressive and amenity issues to concern itself with matters of relief and unemployment.

After approximately 120 years, the founding promise of rural cities has been withdrawn. By accident or design, all three original parties to it have reneged on the deal. Farmers—now only two percent of the U.S. population—are a vanishing breed. Small businesses and shopkeepers are hot on their trail. Ironically, the third party, the mighty metropolitan centers, appear to be having a hard time keeping up with the world they created. This supports the notion developed by Joseph Tainter in *The Collapse of Complex Societies* that complex civilizations decline because they invest too much at their peripheries.

In any case, rural Minnesotans are on the verge of a new admission. They, who took themselves to be full members of an advancing society, are increasingly driven to acknowledge that they are merely the residents of a declining outpost. More and more, their fate resembles that of a colonial people and their civic loyalty is put in question.

At the outset, a warning has to be issued against nostalgia. Abandon any notion that the past was a matter of static communities and fixed identities. Nostalgia overlooks the large role competition, rivalry, failure, resentment, rancor, and hate played in shaping the countryside in the past. With the coming of different ethnic, social, and religious groups to the countryside came mutual suspicion and misunderstanding. Open antagonism often formed a negative axis that marked the affairs of townships and cities with anti-immigrant feelings. These feelings became unusually intense during the First World War. Concerned for national security, local groups spoke out against not just German communities but other non-English speaking communities, such as the Dutch of the Edgerton area. In the 1920s anti-foreign and anti-Catholic sentiments gave birth to chapters of the KKK in rural Minnesota.

Misunderstanding, litigation, and hate (activities not foreign to the human spirit) found a home in the countryside, where almost anything, from the selling of a sick horse . . . to the failure to keep one's fields and ditches clear of weeds . . . to an argument over the grading of roads, could turn neighbor against neighbor. Potential conflicts resided almost everywhere in the countryside—from the laying to the abandoning of a railroad track, the draining of lowlands or lakes to the formation of a farmers' association or a workers' union, which were, and still are, ill-received almost everywhere in rural America.

Cities were part of the spirit of rivalry that filled the countryside. They strongly competed with one another. One city's gain was intuitively—and most often correctly—understood as another's loss. Leaders did not soon forget long struggles to make their town the hub city of the region. They remembered fights to get the county seat, to be the dominant school district, or to house new institutions. In southwest Minnesota there are still sharp recollections of the passionate and guile-filled battles cities fought in the late 1950s and early 1960s to become the site of a new college, Southwest State.

Underlying rivalries between cities—which mirrored and even incorporated earlier township and ethnic rivalries—were also played out more innocently with volunteer fire departments, bands, school teams, Saturday-night fist fights, and Sunday baseball games.

For example, city baseball teams did not hesitate to water down a baseline, freeze balls, or pay professional ringers to get their way on the diamond. There are common stories throughout rural Minnesota of great local teams. (Milroy, Fulda, Ivanhoe, Wanda, Ghent, and Cottonwood were a few of southwest's best.) There are countless stories of great local players who quit the minor leagues because they enjoyed local baseball more and were paid better, too, for playing at home. Old-time fans of what now seems "wild and unregulated baseball" crowded fields by the hundreds and even the thousands for the biggest games. Horns blared late into the night when the hometown team won.

Baseball battles continued energetically from under the lights of the first night leagues in the 1940s well into the late 1950s and 1960s. Smaller towns continually bent their greatest energies to beat the nearby regional center which had outdone them economically but had not conquered them on the magic diamond.

Like baseball, nearly every intercity activity concealed a rivalry, as if there was a mirror on the wall in which community patriots and boosters looked, asking, "who is the greatest town of all?"

Having issued these warnings against nostalgia's tendency to find whole communities and fixed identities in the past, it is, nevertheless, necessary to acknowledge that civic patriotism is in trouble in ways it has never been before.

City governments compete poorly for their citizens' attention, even though their affairs are about such seemingly important matters as civic pride, communal well being, and money. They have done no better than baseball at holding their citizens' interest against television and the plethora of pleasurable activities that have come to the rural world since the 1950s and 1960s.

There is an obvious yet paradoxical reason for the diminished importance of local government. It has grown ever smaller by measure of power, autonomy, and discretion in relation to the worlds beyond it. Yet, at the same time, it has grown too complex—especially in fiscal matters—to captivate and hold the changing interests of its citizenry.

City government is dwarfed by state and federal government. It is increasingly overshadowed by county government which, because of the smaller numbers of counties, has often become the preferred vehicle for state programs in such important regional matters as social services, land control, and pollution. In turn, city and county government are often treated as secondary to the school board, at least by parents whose most important religion is their children's present and future happiness.

Being increasingly powerless in contesting for their pleasure-minded citizens' attention against intrusive outside forces does not exempt city government from acting on such important matters as zoning, policing, downtown revitalization, programs for the elderly, energy codes, housing, industrial development, parks and recreation, tourism, etc. Nor does diminished stature let city government escape the growing complexities of state government or the enhanced aspirations of its citizens. Even the smallest community is driven to rely on outside expertise to try to fulfill its duties.

Matters of taxation, revision of municipal codes, insurance, employee rights and benefits, water and energy supply, and waste and pollution are just some of the complicated issues city governments confront. At accelerating rates, these issues, embedded in complicated laws and complex funding formulas and subject to technical and philosophical debate, exceed the interest and intelligence of all but the most acute and interested local citizens. Here, as everywhere else in society, the complexity of government threatens to demoralize citizens who find themselves required to accept and do what they neither want, nor understand, nor are able to pay for.

Already by the 1970s many of the smallest towns responded to the larger and more complicated world of government by hiring city managers. Recently these administrators have been forced to depend on more distant administrators to understand what is happening to them, what it means, and what they must do about it.

Like a fading star in ever-greater void, city government recedes from its citizens. Civic patriotism wanes as St. Paul and Washington write a text too complicated to be deciphered locally.

The growing fragmentation of the former governing class—the class of small business owners—also contributes to the eclipse of local government and civic patriotism. Even a regional center like Marshall, for example, does not have a single businessperson on its city council. There are similar reports of a vanishing business class in other major regional centers in Minnesota and South Dakota. There appears no evidence from Marshall, Worthington, or even St. Cloud to argue that the new, growing, and often mobile group of citizens composed of state employees, local teachers, and representatives of outside companies are presently in the process of composing themselves into a new class of leaders.

The business class and the epoch of civic patriotism have gone the way of the popularity of town baseball. As the business class surrendered the reins of power over local government during the past decades, citizens distanced themselves from city affairs. Although individual citizens or groups of citizens might kick up dust over specific issues, the overall course of city affairs no longer attracts great passion. Civic identity is no longer a primary identity. Increasingly, the majority of rural citizens, like their fellow Americans, take up the new, manifold, and multiplying identities that—as Stephen Bender argues in *Community and Social Change in America*—make modern society what it is.

Rural people, whose ancestors made great migrations to come to the Minnesota prairie, are again mobile in body and mind. Farmers retire to villages and towns; community dwellers drive to nearby cities to work, to shop, and to take their children to school; and, in turn, the richer citizens of lead cities travel to yet larger and more distant cities for the sake of business, health, new tastes, and fashions. Rural identities are associated with seasonal vacation and retirement patterns.

As baseball went from being a pickup game played by township teams in pastures to an organized sport played on the more carefully manicured diamonds of cities under the rules of a state league, so the people and everything they do have become a matter of greater distances, greater rules and laws, and more distant regional identities.

In conjunction with changing regional, state, and national society, rural people assemble themselves in new associations and communities, and configure their identities accordingly. They do what their ancestors did before they came to settle the prairie: they lend their minds and passion to more distant hopes and imagined worlds. In this manner they transform themselves into migrants and change rural Minnesota from a permanent home to a way station on their own and their family's passage across time.

Announcing the eclipse of civic political identity in rural Minnesota does not mean despair about all communities and identities. People find community in, and have an identity with, their hometowns for all sorts of reasons other than economic growth. There are many things that join a person to a place: including infinite and intangible personal reasons (like one's first kiss, or the crazy squint of a cagey old neighbor) as well as singular places, clubs, groups, and those countless informal associations such as a men's hunting group, a favorite Sunday restaurant, and the local coffee klatch whose gossip and pecking order more or less keep all in their places.

Decline, furthermore, does not stop inhabitants from feeling good about themselves. Newcomers to the region, who most often are from the middle class, commonly find reason to be here and find satisfactory identity in their new jobs. Initially, they are most preoccupied with making themselves and their families at home, whereas the afterglow of the "good old days" lightens the minds of many long-time residents. Living by memory of former accomplishments, they still take pride in recent accomplishments like a new fire hall, a flower garden in the park, or a new multiple-purpose senior center.

Traditional institutions and associations maintain citizens' sense of community and identity in the countryside. Often unobserved in this regard is the importance of ethnic groups which, in any given area, might have successfully built a church, shaped a township, or formed the basis of a cooperative, a telephone exchange, or a chapter of a farm association. In many regions of rural Minnesota, ethnic groups like the Norwegians, Swedes, Germans, Dutch, Belgians, Poles, Czechs, Danes, and others succeeded in transforming a part of this land into communities far more secure, familiar, and economically vigorous than those they had left behind in Europe.

Church is singularly important in making rural Minnesota home for its inhabitants. It baptizes the young, buries the dead, blesses fields, raises high and impressive steeples, runs schools, and does much else that is vital for establishing a primary community.

Other important associations maintaining and extending community are the school, the volunteer fire department, cooperatives of all sorts, farm and civic associations, youth and senior clubs, political parties, and sports and leisure activities—ranging from car racing, baseball, softball, and bowling teams to golf, archery, and karate clubs to chapters of Pheasants Forever.

Although particular civic identities weaken, new, though yet inchoate, regional identities emerge. In contrast to city dwellers, many farmers' senses of community and identity always went beyond a single village. As John Radzilowski illustrates in the case of the Poles and Danes of Lincoln County in his *Out on the Wind*, from the beginning immigrant settlers found themselves in considerable numbers going to one city for church and sociability, and another for market and business. Other factors also stimulated farmers to broaden their identities beyond a single city. The more reliable their automobiles became, the further farmers and farm families traveled from home. The more their brothers and sisters, retired parents, children and cousins, ethnic kinfolk, and neighbors took up residence in nearby townships, villages, counties, and regional centers, the more their sense of identity extended to the region as a whole. Farm organizing, organizing for electrification, and defining watershed districts were some of the many steps that extended farmers' allegiances.

No doubt with more emotional hesitation, inhabitants of the small towns followed the same paths of migration farmers did. As their stores closed and their schools and newspapers were merged, with ever greater frequency they piled into their cars to go to the nearby city for work, business, medical services, entertainment, or "just for the heck of it." New migrations meant new identities.

Throughout rural Minnesota, regional communities and identities associated with work, leisure, learning, aging, health, and care of the elderly are on the rise. Even though these identities have yet to surface in regional political associations and coalitions, there is an increasing movement toward regional identities. Regional centers themselves are filled with representatives of surrounding towns. Life within these centers is a constant source of regional reunions.

Despite decline, the fabric of community is remarkably close. Conversations are always connected and attached to place, and even when the worth of gossip is discounted, they are remarkably particular and wonderfully specific about shared things, places, and people. The sense of being embedded is a great good in this era of impersonal forces and great change. It weighs heavily in the balance of affection and loyalty, community and identity, even if it is light on the scales of career and opportunity.

Nevertheless, as if one can only ascend toward the truth by switchbacks, decline penetrates even the most traditional communities and identities. Traditional churches, such as the Catholic, Lutheran, Presbyterian, and Methodist, all feel the consequences of declining numbers. The New Ulm Diocese of the Catholic Church, for example, has closed ten churches in the last ten years as a consequence of changing demography. It also faces the problem of a severe shortage of priests. (According to official predictions for the New Ulm diocese, there will only be 46 priests in the year 2005.)

The Lutheran church too faces the problems of a declining and an aging population of believers. It closes churches and loses income as the old die and the young donate and sacrifice less than their parents and grandparents did. The financial stress of the church leads many ministers, ironically, to refer to themselves as CEOs—chief economic officers. The weakening of the social fabric and the family force them into the role of social workers and psychologists.

The fundamental communities of work and family also feel the effects of decline. Mirroring the nation, well-paid jobs are in short supply. Family farming remains a viable way of life only for the few and, for many, only on the condition of a spouse's willingness to work off the farm. Small-town business is not much better.

Significantly, rural people now almost universally recognize that families—at least for the great majority—can't be maintained across generations. Parents acknowledge that their children must leave the region for more opportunities, while they themselves, in considerable numbers, recognize that they are but one blue slip away from having to go elsewhere to work and live. One city official in southwest Minnesota speculated that the essential difference between living in a city in the vicinity of the Twin Cities and living in a city in rural Minnesota is the degree to which people are likely, or unlikely, to find other employment if they lose their present jobs.

In short, asking a question that touches the matters of community and identity in the whole nation: How do you put down roots where there is no long-term promise of work or home? Increasingly, rural Minnesota is a place one is more likely to leave than to stay.

How should the people of rural Minnesota compose themselves to live with decline? They might wish to console themselves with stories, not stories of permanent homes but of continuing migrations. These stories do not deny attachment to places; nor do they turn away from people's responsibility for their own well being. However, stories do something that every person, family, and region should: they explain people's experiences.

Beyond this, they should not expect too much from their city or their civic patriotism. The politics of cities, as Bender noted, "is more likely to be public than communal, and there is nothing wrong with this." They must free public life, and the political process and culture associated with it, from the hope that it will provide them with a whole community and a single identity.

Furthermore, by failing to recognize that the people of rural Minnesota are but a small and flagging region of a great, expanding, and contradictory market, nation, and world, they simply expect too much from politics and run the risk of discouragement. They can respect the region's communities, accomplishments, and diversity; they can insist on making the best of their condition. They should not expect, if they value their sanity, to feel at home in a world whose great forces assure no one lasting community or enduring progress.

CHAPTER FOUR

The Changing of the Guard

As early as the 1960s the councils and mayors of rural cities, even some with populations less than a thousand inhabitants, began to hire city managers to help them govern. By the early 1970s, new city managers, who were appearing in even greater numbers in the countryside, were expected to have a college degree related to city planning. By the late 1970s they assumed their position on the basis of having credentials that defined them as professionally trained city administrators.

The appearance of professional city managers in the countryside is not surprising. They are a result of a world in which specialization occurs in all things, and professionals replace amateurs in all phases of human activity. In this new and emerging world, specialization grows at a more rapid pace than the population itself.

Rural leaders are left doing more with less. Correspondingly, rural veterinarians, doctors, and lawyers (to choose only three examples) who practiced their professions alone now commonly form themselves into firms while, at the same time, whole new professions—like family counselors, trust agents, and travel agents—appear in regional lead cities to meet rural peoples' expanding needs and wants.

It is no accident that professional city managers began to appear in the countryside in the same period that rural audiences transferred their support from local to professional baseball, farmers were forced to spend more time ploughing with pencils rather than tractors, and rural shoppers traveled greater distances to secure larger varieties of goods. By hiring professional city managers, traditional city leaders acknowledged that a new era of professionalism had arrived in the countryside and, in effect, confessed that they could no longer manage their own affairs.

This change mirrored the transformation of rural America and its institutions. Hospitals, schools, and churches closed, merged, or joined consortiums as they were forced to meet growing legal requirements and the need for new and expanded services. Co-ops, banks, savings and loans, and insurance companies followed suit. In hiring professionals, rural governments of amateurs were just keeping up with public and private boards which hired more and more executive directors and professional staffs to keep apace of society at large.

This new breed of professional city managers, who arrived on the scene approximately twenty to thirty years ago, were part of a national transformation that saw the demise of the age of the amateur and the republic give way to empire. These new professional governmental managers were expected to make sense of this great transformation. They were asked to do the impossible: to revitalize the old and to prepare the new.

The traditional leaders of towns and cities wanted them to resuscitate what was moribund. The dominant local business class, a class on the wane, wanted them to produce a thriving economy. Mayors and council members, bowled over by the new complexities of law and want, expected them to simplify precisely those things that state and federal government were in the process of making complex.

Local government was more complicated than it ever had been before. A brief historical taxonomy of government functions indicates its accumulating complexity. In the period 1870–1890, local government was preoccupied with private development, platting, government organization, and roads. In the period 1890–1910 it was concerned with fire and police protection, and nuisances. From 1910 to 1930 it was caught up with utility construction and park development, which included city baseball fields and, occasionally, municipal golf courses and race tracks. In the period 1930–1950 it dedicated itself to health services and enterprise development. From 1950 to 1970 it hired professional staff while turning its attention to planning and zoning. Since then, imitating larger cities everywhere, it has promoted housing development and set out in quest of the more elusive prizes of economic and community development

These new goals did not relieve the administrators from problems which had made their appearance in rural towns three decades before. They continued to confront decline. They encountered the problems of a shrinking rural population, the migration of the young, an aging population, an absence of good jobs, and a comparative loss of amenities. Due to the severity of the farm crisis of the 1980s, these problems became more severe. In this decade, the most rural regions of Minnesota, where the towns are smallest, experienced truly dramatic population losses, reaching almost 20 percent and causing, in some counties, natural decline.

Joined to these demographic changes were protracted economic problems. Although unemployment has consistently stayed below the national average in rural Minnesota, underemployment—a failure to furnish work equal to a people's abilities and needs—remains endemic. As family income falters and government dependency increases in rural Minnesota, there is a growing underclass whose interest in public life diminishes as its dependency grows.

Managers of local government are also confronted by problems caused by declining real estate values. The depreciation of property below its mortgage value results in a mounting loss of economic power and flexibility on the part of rural citizens and feeds a pervasive pessimism. Nurtured by a sense of being trapped in an economic backwater, this pessimism vents itself on local government whose managers are ready scapegoats.

Compounding the managers' problems is the steady disappearance of traditional leaders and the main-street business class. The exodus of traditional leaders anticipates a profound changing of the guard. So far no new order of leaders has emerged, or has even been defined. Instead, city governments, who have not yet tapped the potential of new residents and women for leadership, flounder. Government is presently formed by provisional and shifting groups of individuals whose passion about a single issue matches a lack of historical perspective or long-term goals. Frequently, they define nothing more than a politics of reaction and resentment, an angry politics. This brand of politics is unpredictable; worse, it is composed of half-baked ideas, shifting emotions, and changing people.

The managers receive no direction from outside agencies either. Federal programs remain a maze through which they must thread their way. The erratic pace of state legislation and its changing and inconsistent funding formulae increasingly turn local government into a topsy-turvy affair. Neither public nor private agencies can be expected even to prescribe a way out of this condition.

It is little wonder that astute managers have grown weary of the idea of rural development. They see it as far more a matter of hope than a clear science or an applied art. Aside from serving its proponents' wallets and emotional needs, city leaders can critically judge rural development—or at least most schemes promising it—as a surrender to false expectations. Rural development's grandiose ideas and ambitions can undercut such modest but important achievements as building a new water system, starting an ice rink, or paving a road. Worse, they can turn managers and their colleagues into "program junkies," constantly in need of a new developmental gimmick to give them a high to escape the cramped and meager possibilities of everyday city life.

City managers grow cynical. Despite their best efforts, some cannot escape the fact that they work for fragmented communities and stick-in-the-mud leaders. They recognize that they can fall victim to drastic and precipitous shifts of opinions of city councils. Almost from the first day in town, city managers report, they are asked to work magic, while continuing to be treated as outsiders long after they have come to town. Invariably, they must keep their finger in the air, for new and better jobs are rarely any longer just down the road.

What is particularly discouraging for many managers is the recognition that they, like the whole rural world, belong to a team that has been losing far more than winning for the last several decades. They feel like custodians of a failing enterprise. While winning no exemption from the requirement of trying to do more with less, they live in a climate saturated with a sense of stalemate and retreat. The towns they head, which once prided themselves on being on the forefront of civilization's advance, now console themselves by pointing out things they have not lost or managed to regain.

Rural leaders often find themselves without a community to lead. They govern a void of energy and interest. The well-off increasingly follow their own pleasures and pursuits, while others are increasingly dependent on government services and programs. They see their towns filled with more of those who are less responsible for themselves. Accordingly, finding themselves increasingly reduced to govern by administering mandated dependency payments, they see themselves more and more as keepers of rural wards of the state.

It is apparent to many managers that city government must

quit doing as much as it does. Inside its jurisdiction it must work much more closely with schools, medical facilities, and utilities. Outside it, city governments must pair services, such as police protection, with county governments. They must share water and sewer with rural water systems, and join administration with other communities. City governments must experiment with new forms of technologies to reduce the cost of government and business, expand productivity, and provide new job opportunities. Finally, they must recognize that their good may depend on government dedicating funds and attention to what is strongest, not what is weakest.

This does not save city managers and leaders from having to learn to live with resignation. They must resign themselves to the fact that the countryside, like American society as a whole, will continue to be driven by powerful world market forces which are oblivious to smaller communities and require multiple, irregular, and often contradictory interventions of state and national governments. These interventions will frequently prove to be antithetical to small rural communities. They also must acknowledge that agriculture, the founding and sustaining industry of the countryside, will support fewer and fewer people on the land. (A "cheap food" policy will in all likelihood remain the standing and irrevocable policy of the federal government.) They must realize that the discrepancies in employment opportunities and amenities between rural and urban centers profoundly favor migration. Furthermore, they must resign themselves to having to continue to confront a maze of state and federal laws and agencies that impose contradictory, arbitrary, and expensive obligations across the whole spectrum of rural life. Finally, they cannot avoid the singularly paradoxical demand of their own rural citizens who continue to want amenities that they, as taxpayers, don't want to pay for. They continue to want to starve the goose they expect to lay golden eggs.

Although fashionable prescriptions, regimes, and even quasi-spiritualities for rural revitalization abound, rural leaders will have to resign themselves to the fact that real cures are scarce. If any one thing pushes regional leaders to recognize limits to reform, it is the number and size of attacks that exist against rural self-determination. Rural citizens are more and more likely to be recipients rather than producers of wealth as the value of assets and the tax base in declining towns shrink. Regional revenues as a whole are increasingly dependent on the transfer of state and federal funds. Only twenty percent of the money under the control of city government comes directly from property taxes. The remainder comes in the form of mandated funds that are not subject to local discretion. Even if the favorable ratio of transfer of funds continues—which is highly unlikely given the shift of the state's population to the suburbs—rural leaders find themselves in a condition similar to leaders of an undeveloped country: their people are fed and kept, while their products and children are taken.

Minnesota's rural leaders face a long-standing problem faced by democratic leaders of impoverished rural regions throughout the world. They must seek to transform fragmented and dependent rural populations into a self-determining people. Defying the flow of things, they must seek to involve citizens in government affairs that are beyond local control. In effect, they must do the impossible: ask their citizens to understand and alter what is incomprehensible and inalterable. They must teach the value of independence in a world whose primary lessons are about dependence.

Civic dependency and the sense of fatalism joined to it threaten the most important democratic ideal of all: the belief that citizens can shape their own destiny. Such a belief is more than a state of mind or a collective enthusiasm. It does not materialize out of thin air; it cannot be achieved by the recitation of fixed formulae or conjured by motivational tricks. The belief in freedom is as unique, precious, and ephemeral as freedom itself and as rare as great moments of human history born of it.

Rural leaders also must recognize that the course of history has not been set by the deeds of small rural cities. They must acknowledge that prairie towns since their very beginnings have marched to the beat of the distant drums of the metropolitan centers like Chicago, St. Louis, St. Paul, and Minneapolis. Nevertheless, these rural leaders also must recognize that a sense of freedom and self-determination existed in the smallest prairie communities since their beginnings—and their farms, churches, and towns bear the imprint of their hopes, dreams, and self-making.

The elixir of sensing one's own self-determination still belongs to many rural cities, especially those larger growing regional centers that offer amenities and opportunities. This proud identity is born out of possibilities and successes that assemble a community's imagination for new adventures. Indeed, a primary responsibility of regional and civic leaders is to help citizens risk new adventures and tell stories in which they are the primary actors.

The chance for new stories is not absent in the countryside. Its soil is still rich. There is abiding promise in new crops and value-added farm products. Rural populations, aged, enfeebled, are still not without energy and pride. On the whole they are ready to work—and work at lower wages than their urban counterparts—to preserve a way of life they cherish. By virtue of living in a small world, rural citizens have intimate knowledge of and experience in creating things.

Regional lead cities themselves remain a matter of considerable promise. Even though they are short of good jobs, they are more or less keeping pace with metropolitan centers, generally providing good schools and adequate recreational, medical, and shopping facilities. These cities also have an economy of scale and available housing (at least in nearby communities), while offering safety and security. They still offer the stability, familiarity, and sense of community that is highly cherished and increasingly absent in metropolitan centers and their suburbs.

Leaders of rural cities still have a role to play in the countryside worthy of large visions and great risk. If they fail, they fail themselves and the small towns and countryside around them. However, they can do no less than seek to empower their citizens by offering knowledge and choices. They must explain circumstances, simplify options, honestly articulate new projects, and record successes. They must honor their citizens' imagination, will, and memory, while helping make them as free and self-determining as possible.

At the End of a Way

This book is not an argument over the virtues of pessimism and optimism. Instead, it concludes by simply explaining why rural Minnesota is at the end of one way and the beginning of another.

Earlier essays demonstrated the steady decline of the towns and family farms that little more than a hundred years ago grew rapidly and constituted a new civilization on the prairie. The collapse of that civilization is associated with a shrinking and aging population, diminishing economic resources and political influence, the emigration of its youth and its most talented citizens, the decrease of its business class, and the virtual disappearance of the crucial local leaders that class once furnished.

This decline is related to the failure of rural cities to keep up with rising expectations and increasing laws, specialization, and bureaucracies of state and nation. Like its primary associations and institutions—banks, savings and loans, hospitals, co-ops, churches, schools, law firms, insurance companies, and businesses—rural cities are driven to consolidate and surrender their autonomy to distant powers and places. This causes a corresponding loss of self-respect and pride. As native peoples of this region lost their place and way on the land, so their successors (peoples assembled from rural America and Europe) now lose their place and way as they are subject to the increasing encroachments and demands of a specializing civilization. Like rural people throughout the world, they increasingly become the economic, political, and cultural wards of the metropolitan center.

One measure of the eclipse of rural life is the number of regional leaders who neither understand nor defend the varieties of community that exist here. Many of them adopt (for reasons of ignorance or self-interest) the fashionable and state-supported propositions of the metropolis. Ignoring the variety of native people—French-Canadians, Czechs, Poles, Germans, Irish, Belgians, Dutch, Mennonite—and other peoples who made the prairie a rich quilt of peoples, these new critics reduce and homogenize this region's people into being merely the children of white, northern, Protestant Europeans, and assume that cultural diversity began with the recent appearance of Asian and Hispanic workers.

These critics (usually of the urban, liberal, upper-middle class) take no interest in older migrations of workers into our area. Surprisingly, if their interest is truly cultural diversity as they claim, they even ignore the small number of colorful black and Latino baseball players who graced the game in its early stages here and the traveling salesmen, tinkers, tramps, hoboes, and vagabonds as well as the influx of foreign brides from the Second World War and other immigrants from the east and west coasts. More significantly, they overlook the powerful reality of class in the countryside. They ignore the recent and profound transformations of work, crafts, trades, and professions; and revolutionary changes in the practice of rural veterinarians, doctors, lawyers, accountants, pharmacists, and other professions. They are indifferent to the meaning of the recent appearance in regional centers of such specialists as travel agents, family counselors, and financial consultants. They are baffled by rural life and culture.

Indifferent to local details and experiences, these critics, who serve their own agendas that are nationally fashionable, don't even consider the possibility that differences of class and locality might be as important as gender and race. They don't grasp how religion still profoundly shapes regional people's ideas of self, family, and community; exchange, charity, cooperation, and sacrifice; and their views of the dead and afterlife. Religion still accounts for some of the most important divisions in the countryside. Likewise, these urban, upper-middle class critics don't consider important distinctions that exist between old-timers and newcomers, the citizens of small towns and those of regional centers, rich and poor farmers, successful business people and a growing range of city, county, and state employees who have begun to outnumber other classes in rural Minnesota.

Of other distinctions and divisions that go unnoticed, none is as important as those that exist between different generations. Measured by changing technology, there still is a generation in the countryside who knew rural life before the gasoline-driven tractor became prevalent and before electricity lit up the night's darkness, scaring away the spirits, lifting farm pumps, and gracing the insides of farm houses with radios and then televisions which wired the farm to changing and multiplying national tastes and fashions. There are also those who, having lived before the formation of the modern welfare and whole new worlds of social services and dependency, remember a time when the old, the sick, and the abandoned ended up on county poor farms, and poor widows with children received the only meager mother's pensions.

Changes such as these mark great divides in human experience. They cause revolutions in expectations and alter fundamental senses of work, pain, pleasure, space, comfort, home, and self. Encompassing changes continue to permeate the rural world to its core, producing new breeds of individuals and families. There are now even farmers who, linked by home computers to distant markets, no longer have any contact whatsoever with either gardens or animals.

Post-secondary educational institutions—which became part of the rural landscape in the 1960s and 1970s—also profoundly changed rural cultures. Although the effects of these institutions deserve further study, they clearly produced unexpected results. Rather than serving their founders' intentions to stem the exodus of rural youth, they hastened their parting. With increased skills and expectations, students left the countryside for better things and places: The higher a student's educational level, the greater their migrations. Recent dramatic increases in the number of non-traditional students offer further testimony to rural education's function as a vehicle for migration.

Isolation, so crucial to the definition of the traditional rural order, steadily vanishes as the countryside is ever more deeply penetrated by the powers, markets, and ideas of the distant metropolis. To find an analogy in contemporary physic's creation theory, the countryside as a whole is being pulled ever more strongly into the gravitational field of the metropolitan center from which it originated. Having once exploded in a sort of "big bang" out of the center on to the most remote parts of the prairie, the countryside, now cooling, is attracted back, by want and necessity, at a quickening pace to the metropolitan center.

From its beginnings, however, rural life was dominated by the center. In a matter of two decades, the land was subordinated to distant markets. Railroads established a new grid on the landscape, discarding the river as the first road of settlement and transportation and a source of the ecological system that had defined life on the prairie since time immemorial. With the coming of the settlers, the Indian, the buffalo, the elk, and the wolf (the most traditional rural symbol of wilderness) were removed from rural Minnesota. By the 1890s the last wolf bounties were paid in southwestern Minnesota. (The last official wolf bounty in Lyon County was paid in the sum of $80 in 1896 to Eugene Knox who produced the scalps of 16 wolf cubs and averred in his "oath of claimant for wolf bounty," as all bounty hunters were required, "he did not spare the life of any wolf that it was within his power to kill.")

As happened to the world's great prairies—in Siberia, on the Argentine pampas, and in North America—fields became factories. A handful of plants (first wheat, then corn, and later soybeans) and a few animals (horses, cows, and pigs) came to dominate. Others became interlopers. Unwanted plants became weeds, unneeded animals and insects, pests. Water, too, was taken in hand. Lowlands, in their great variety of marshes, sloughs, and shallow lakes, were drained in the name of land reclamation. Drainage ditches, begun before the First World War, laid the basis for a new epoch of water control after the Second World War when, for economic reasons, fields were tiled and farms were planted from fence row to fence row.

As the new civilization, characterized by railroad towns and farmers' symmetrical fields, dominated the prairie, so the new settlers tamed themselves. They took control of their education, tongues, and bodies. They built schools and churches, got indoor water and took more frequent baths, looked at themselves in mirrors, installed glass cases to display their valuables, got electricity, bought vacuum cleaners to suck up dust, took to wearing fancy-colored shirts and skirts, had themselves vaccinated to fight the terrible smallpox, and carried out more elaborate funerals and burials to elevate and honor their loved ones beyond the soil they worked. They took to labor-saving devices almost as quickly as they appeared, fought for electricity for their homes, and sent their children for more years of schooling and, in accord with the nation's growing acceptance of leisure, they belatedly let them stay at school to play more and more sports and try their hand at plays. They drove cars to distant villages to see new movies and took to listening to far away baseball teams. In southern and southwest Minnesota, it was first the Cubs and only later the Twins. In time, local baseball lost almost all its fans to television screens.

The people of the countryside steadily entangled themselves with distant public institutions. They had the insane in their families carted off to St. Peter, and later Willmar; they listened to state public health officers regarding themselves and their animals; and poignantly, in the case of the large German population of southwest Minnesota, during the First World War they let their sons be turned into American soldiers to fight cousins and brothers in the old country.

The most cunning individuals and ethnic groups in the countryside learned to calculate the advantages and disadvantages of their affairs. They formed co-ops, associations, and organizations to secure better prices, to insure themselves against fires, and to deal with distant markets and lobby state and national capitols. They discovered that they could not survive and prosper without keeping their eyes on the city. Through a changing mixture of choice and necessity, they wove themselves into the fabric of state and nation and, in this manner, citizens of towns and ethnic farmers transformed themselves into Minnesotans and Americans.

In truth, rural farms and cities were never as autonomous as they were depicted. Time proved them to be less and less so. Neither a place on a prospering farm nor a secure niche in the town's community exempted anyone from national markets and fashions. The towns and the land were settled by many here as means to obtaining the wealth and the benefits of an expanding civilization. Already in the 1890s settlers abandoned their farms and villages as the value of crops fell and drought overtook the land. Patterns of migration from the countryside, alternatively driven by necessity and want, can be observed since then.

Since the founding of the region, rural youth has left the countryside for better opportunities in the city. In the last few decades, the old themselves migrate in increasing numbers as they choose lower taxes, better health care, and fun in the sun. Migration shapes all facets of contemporary rural culture. Grandparents, parents, and grandchildren travel ever greater distances to meet. Their journeys define new perspectives in the meaning of self and family, region, nation, and world.

Like the rural people of the world, the rural people of Minnesota increasingly perceive themselves as migrants rather than settled peoples. They know themselves not by a fixed homeland but by stories of their migrations. The myth of the countryside's permanence is surrendered.

The traditional way is at an end. This order already belongs more to the past than the future. The farmer's dominance of the region is over; the leadership of the small business class is done for; increasingly rural Minnesota is culturally dominated by outsiders. Even many of those who remain in body have emigrated in mind; they have made themselves full members of commercial and national cultures.

The civilization that arose on the prairie has proven to be brief and provisional. The center, which clearly cannot control or direct itself, imposes its mounting powers, laws, and appetites on the countryside. It intrudes, reorders, changes, and finally obliterates traditional rural ethnic cultures. The new relationships and cultures that result from this immense encroachment are yet to be defined and studied. Future historians will struggle with this.

The transformation of rural Minnesota during the last one hundred twenty-five years mirrors the history of the countryside across the world. For those who are truly interested in cultural diversity, the transformation of the old world must be studied. The new leaders of the countryside will not teach us to value ourselves solely as the children of settled people or heirs of a fixed tradition, but the inheritors of a courageous lineage of migration and adaptation. We have given lie to the old truth, "Man makes the city; God, the countryside." We must give life to the new truth that we truly are at the end of one way and the beginning another.

Bibliography

In addition to information from the Bureau of the Census for 1950, 1960, 1970, 1980, and 1990, statistical information was provided by the U.S. Department of Commerce, Vital Statistics Division; the Minnesota Department of Health; State Demographers Office, State of Minnesota; and the National Center for Health Statistics of the U.S. Department of Health and Human Services.

Also of statistical use were Felicity Barringer, "Where Many Elderly Live," *The New York Times*, March 7, 1993; Daniel Elazar, *Cities of the Prairie Revisited* (Lincoln: University of Nebraska Press, 1986); Robert Heil, "Exodus . . . People in Flight," summarized and published as a series by Lew Hudson in the Worthington Daily Globe, October 18–24, 1971; Robert Holloway, *A City is More than People: A Study of Fifteen Minnesota Communities* (Minneapolis: University of Minnesota Press, 1954); Barclay Jones, *The Rural-Urban Balance Reconsidered: New Trends in Population Distribution* (Ithaca: Cornell University Press, 1979); R. W. Murchie and M. E. Jarchow, *Population Trends in Minnesota*, Bulletin No. 32 (University of Minnesota Agricultural Experiment Station, 1936); Lowry Nelson et al., *A Century of Population Growth in Minnesota* (St. Paul: Agricultural Experiment Station, University of Minnesota, 1953); eds. Vic Spadaccini and Susan Becker, *Minnesota Pocket Data Book,*

1985–1986 (Minneapolis: Blue Sky Marketing, 1985–86); Andrew Sofranko and James D. Williams, *Rebirth of Rural America: Rural Migration in the Midwest* (Ames: Iowa State University Press, 1980); Linda Swanson, *What Attracts New Residents to Nonmetro Areas?* (Washington, D.C.: USDA, 1986).

Essential for our work were the writings of University of Minnesota geographer John Borchert, especially, *America's Northern Heartland* (Minneapolis: University of Minnesota Press, 1987) and "The Urban Centers" (unpublished manuscript, nd., pp. 59). Also, important in providing a framework for understanding the new civilization formed by the railroads was John Hudson, *Plains Country Towns* (Minneapolis: University of Minnesota Press, 1985), and William Cronon, *Nature's Metropolis: Chicago and the Great West* (New York: Norton, 1991). For the relationship between the center and peripheries of a civilization, see Joseph A. Tainter's *The Collapse of Complex Societies* (Cambridge: Cambridge University Press, 1988). For a recent demographic speech confirming our basic analysis, see Mark Drabenstott, vice president and economist for the Federal Reserve Bank of Kansas City, "Prospects for Rural Prosperity in the 1990s," presented to the Farm Credit Council annual meeting, San Antonio, January 26, 1993.

For a short history of the League of Cities, see "International Falls Convention Will Mark League's Silver Anniversary," *Minnesota Municipalities*, June, 1938, 188–194, and "Fifty Years of Service to Municipal Government," *Minnesota Municipalities*, January and June, 1963, 4–7, 68–71.

For a few suggestive books on rural decline, see Joseph Amato, *The Great Jerusalem Artichoke Circus: The Buying and Selling of the Rural American Dream* (Minneapolis: University of Minnesota Press, 1993) and *When Father and Son Conspire: A Minnesota Farm Murder* (Ames: Iowa State University Press, 1988); Osha Davidson, *Broken Heartland: Rise of America's Ru-*

ral Ghetto (New York: The Free Press, 1990); Gilbert Fite, *American Farmers: The New Minority* (Bloomington: Indiana University Press, 1981); Michael Lesy, *Wisconsin Death Trip* (New York: Random House, 1973); Don Martindale and R. Galen Hanson, *Small Town and the Nation: The Conflict of Local and Translocal Forces* (Westport, Conn.: Greenwood Press, 1969); Jane Marie Pederson, *Between Memory and Reality: Family and Community in Rural Wisconsin, 1870–1970* (Madison: University of Wisconsin Press, 1992); Richard Rodefeld, ed., *Rural America: Causes, Consequences, and Alternatives* (Saint Louis: C. V. Mosby, 1978).

Two works of several from French history which influenced our conception of decline were André Varagnac, *Civilisation traditionelle et genres de vie* (Paris: Albin Michel, 1948), and Eugen Weber, *Peasants into Frenchmen: The Modernization of Rural France, 1879-1914* (Stanford: Stanford University Press, 1976). Of continuing inspiration are the works of Guy Thuillier, most recently, *Histoire locale et régionale* (Paris: Presses Universitaires de France, 1992).

For the settlement of peoples in Minnesota, see Joseph Amato, *Servants of the Land: God, Family, and Farm, The Trinity of Belgian Economic Folkways in Southwestern Minnesota* (Marshall, Minnesota: Crossings Press, 1990); Theodore Blegen, *Minnesota. A History of the State* (Minneapolis: University of Minnesota Press, 1963); Clark Clifford, ed., *Minnesota in a Century of Change: The State and Its People* (St. Paul: Minnesota Historical Society Press, 1989); Rhoda Gillman, *The Story of Minnesota's Past* (St. Paul: Minnesota Historical Society Press, 1989); June Holmquist, ed., *They Chose Minnesota: A Survey of the State's Ethnic Groups* (St. Paul: Minnesota Historical Society Press, 1981); Robert Ostergren, *A Community Transplanted: The Trans-Atlantic Experience of a Swedish Immigrant Settlement in the Upper Middle West, 1835–1915* (Madison: University of Wisconsin Press, 1988); John Radzilowski, *Out on the Wind: Poles and Danes in Lincoln County, 1880–1905* (Marshall, Minnesota: Crossings Press, 1992).

Of historiographical use are four pamphlets published by Marshall's Society for the Study of Local and Regional History in their Historical Essays on Rural Life, Tim Kolhei, "From Dusty Trails to Rusty Rails: The Rise and Fall of Hanley Falls, Minnesota"; Odd Lovoll's "Norwegians on the Land" (1992); Robert Schoone-Jongen's "Patriotic Pressures, WWI, The Dutch Experience in Southwest Minnesota During World War I" (1992); and Robert Swierenga's "The Dutch Transplanting in the Upper Middle West" (1991).

About the Authors

Joseph Amato

Joseph Amato is a professor of history and the director of rural studies at Southwest State University in Marshall, Minnesota. He also is an active member of the Society for the Study of Local and Regional History and stimulated many of its publications. Aside from book and articles in European history and philosophy, his own multiple publications include *Countryside: Mirror of Ourselves; When Father and Son Conspire: A Study of a Minnesota Farm Murder; Servants of the Land: God, Family, and Farm, The Trinity of Belgian Economic Folkways in Southwestern Minnesota; A New College on the Prairie: Southwest State University's First Twenty-Five Years, 1967–1992;* and most recently, *The Great Jerusalem Artichoke Circus: The Buying and Selling of the Rural American Dream* (University of Minnesota Press, Fall, 1993), which is a study of an incident from the early 1980s which involved the selling of twenty-five million of the Jerusalem artichoke tuber-seed to twenty-five hundred farmers in the United States and Canada as a God-given answer to their problems. He is presently at work on additional studies in regional and local history.

John W. Meyer

John Meyer is an applied sociologist, specializing in public management and finance. He has researched, designed, and managed several significant public development projects in rural Minnesota. With an M.S. in Geography and a Ph.D. in Rural Sociology from South Dakota State University, he is author of 19 critical cultural/demographic reports and three development simulation computer software applications. He is currently engaged in research for a series of articles on the impact of development attempts in rural Minnesota.

◆

The Decline of Rural Minnesota was typeset in 10/14.2 New Century Schoolbook type. Design and production by Kathy Wenzel of the Livewire Printing Company, 310 Second Street, P.O. Box 208, Jackson, MN 56143.

◆